REFUGEES

Seeking a Safe Haven

Kem Knapp Sawyer

—Multicultural Issues—

ENSLOW PUBLISHERS, INC.

44 Fadem Road   P.O. Box 38

Box 699   Aldershot

Springfield, N.J. 07081   Hants GU12 6BP

U.S.A.   U.K.

Library of Congress Cataloging-in-Publication Data

Sawyer, Kem Knapp.
    Refugees: seeking a safe haven / by Kem Knapp Sawyer.
        p. cm. – (Multicultural issues)
    Includes bibliographical references and index.
    Summary: Discusses the problems that refugees face and the efforts
of the international community to stem the tide of refugees.
    ISBN 0-89490-663-1
    1. Refugees–Juvenile literature. [1. Refugees.] I. Title.
    II. Series.
    JV6346.R4S29   1995
    362.87–dc20

                                                            94-41425
                                                                CIP
                                                                 AC

Printed in the United States of America

10 9 8 7 6 5 4 3 2

Illustration Credits: Luka Dugajlia/Croatian Information Center, p. 96; Richard Howard, p. 33; Kluger/Central Zionist Archive, Jerusalem, Israel, courtesy of the United States Holocaust Memorial Museum, p. 24; Jeff MacNelly/reprinted by permission: Tribune Media Services, p. 47; Mwiza Munthali/TransAfrica Forum, p. 51; National Archives, Washington D.C., courtesy of the United States Holocaust Memorial Museum, p. 109; Kem Knapp Sawyer, p. 101; UNHCR/M. Amar, p. 62; UNHCR/D. Bregnard, p. 43; UNHCR/A. Hollmann, pp. 8, 31, 60, 78, 90, 94; UNHCR/M. Kobayashi, p. 83; UNHCR/P. Moumtzis, p. 57; UNHCR/L. Taylor, p. 86; UNRWA/H. Haider, p. 72; UNRWA/Z. Mazskian, p. 69; YIVO Institute for Jewish Research, New York, courtesy of the United States Holocaust Memorial Museum, p. 21.

Cover Illustration: Odell Mitchell, Jr./*St. Louis Post Dispatch*

Contents

Acknowledgments

I would like to thank Francis Deng, United Nations representative of the secretary-general on internally displaced persons, as well as Judy Mayotte and Lynn Kneedler of Refugees International for sharing their knowledge and expertise. For their contributions and their help in procuring illustrations, I also thank Odell Mitchell from the *St. Louis Post Dispatch* for the cover photo; Tom Argent, Virginia Hamilton, and Koula Papanicolas at the U.S. Committee for Refugees; Andrew Campana and Vivian Boxer at the U.S. Holocaust Memorial Museum; Heather Courtney from the Office of the United Nations High Commissioner for Refugees; Liz Heath at the Corcoran School of Art; Myrna Jurcev from the Croatian Information Center; photographer Richard Howard; Tien Van Le and Judy Poulin at the Refugee Service Center; and Mwiza Munthali at TransAfrica.

Leaving Home

———————⊕———————

A refugee lives in the midst of uncertainty. A man must desert his home not knowing if or when he will see it again. If he were to return to his native land, he might find his home and all that was once his destroyed. A woman carries a baby on her back as she too abandons familiar surroundings. The clothes she wears may be the only ones she owns. A child, no longer attending school, leaves behind those who once were friends. For many, food is scarce and medical attention hard to come by. A refugee lives from day to day in a world that has no guarantees . . . .

"We just want to be given a chance to live as human beings, at least to die as human beings," Rasija Tanovic, a Bosnian woman, told *Washington Post* reporter David Ottaway in February 1994. She and her daughter hid in a dark basement of a shell-battered apartment building in Mostar, an ancient city in Bosnia, besieged by Croats. Twelve other families lived with them, sleeping in the same room and taking turns cooking, eating, and washing in a small entrance hall on the ground floor. They were "living like rats," Jerrie Hulem, a United Nations (UN) relief official, said. They subsist without clean water or electricity. "Is the world informed about our plight?" Tanovic asked. "Do they know we haven't had any toothpaste, hygienic items or new clothes for 10 months? No potatoes, onions, not even powdered eggs or milk. Do they know?" Tanovic spent a year in these conditions living essentially as a prisoner with 55,000 others, mostly Muslims, in the Old City of Mostar.[1]

Millions of people around the world have lost the freedom to remain in their homes or choose where they want to live. Some leave a country divided by war. Others are oppressed because of their religion, political beliefs, or skin color. Forced to flee, refugees cross the border into another country in search of peace and security. The United Nations has estimated that the number of refugees reached 19.7 million in November of 1993. One out of every 125 people in this world is a refugee.

For many refugees, finding a new home is a long, tedious, and painful process. They spend months, and even years, in temporary quarters. "Living in a refugee center cannot be called 'life,' either. It's more like living in a big waiting room," said Jadranka Hadzalic, a Bosnian refugee.[2] The High Commission for Refugees, created by the United Nations to protect refugees, helps refugees with integration into a new society. This commission also works to change the conditions in the country of origin so that refugees may return to their homes—a process called repatriation.

Many host countries that receive refugees suffer from overpopulation, housing shortages, and rising unemployment. An influx of refugees only increases problems that already exist. In addition, these countries cannot meet additional demands on their already beleaguered health care and educational systems. Although many governments recognize that they have a responsibility to protect refugees, they feel challenged not only by limited space and the lack of funds to meet basic needs but also by the difficulties in distinguishing between immigrants and refugees. Those who seek better economic opportunities but have not suffered from persecution are frequently confused with refugees. They receive many of the same benefits and often drain a country's resources so that little remains for those who are truly refugees. Increasingly, governments are demanding that those who seek protection be subjected to a fair process that welcomes refugees but does not permit the voluntary migration of those who have not been forced to flee.

Refugees are driven to flight for a variety of reasons, such as insecurity resulting from living in an unstable country where violence is rampant or fear for the safety of one's family in a war-torn country. Threats to human rights may often precipitate flight. Frequently, refugees have suffered in a country where the government denies its people basic freedoms, including freedom of speech or religion. They flee when the government takes away their right to assemble

Women from a camp for displaced persons in Azerbaijan, formerly part of the USSR. Violence within the country caused 500,000 to become homeless in 1993.

peaceably, to receive a fair trial, to own property, to belong to a political party, or to travel within a country or outside it. They flee to escape torture or imprisonment by a brutal government.

"Some of today's worst refugee crises might have been prevented had the will and the way existed to respond to clear warnings that massive human rights violations were occurring or were imminent," says Reed Brody, executive director of the International Human Rights Law Group.[3] The High Commission for Refugees works to assure that governments respect the human rights of all citizens.

The United Nations and other international organizations respond to the immediate needs of people by providing food, water, shelter, and medical care. They also apply pressure on other countries to provide asylum or protection. Many humanitarian organizations that work with refugees realize that although they must provide immediate relief for the survival of the refugees, they must also give more far-reaching assistance to ease their plight. In search of long-term solutions, the Women's Commission for Refugee Women and Children strives to empower refugees to become self-reliant:

> From the first moment a refugee crosses a border, he or she needs food and shelter—this is relief. But from this moment, each refugee needs much more—and this is development. Relief and development are worlds apart. Trauma needs relief, but living demands development. Relief leads to dependency; development is empowering and champions self-sufficiency.[4]

Members of the international community, including the United Nations and other organizations, seek to provide a stable environment where men and women may pursue their work, raise families, and educate their children. To make this happen, they often must first help end famine, ethnic strife, or civil war. Preventing a flood of refugees can sometimes involve correcting economic imbalances, alleviating poverty, or halting arms proliferation. Roger Winter, director of the U.S. Committee for Refugees, has called for the de-weaponization of the world, from Angola to Central Asia to southeast Washington, D.C. He believes that "making the UN effective, responding to the worldwide law and order deficit, reducing the availability of weapons (big and small) [will] affect the lot of future refugees and displaced people far more than all the relief supplies our minds can conceive."[5]

Those who work with refugees are pulled in many directions. They often must choose between providing emergency aid or putting their energy and resources into preventing a refugee crisis. Finding the proper balance can be a difficult and controversial task.

Although the international community places a great emphasis on changing the conditions that create a refugee flow, Sadako Ogata, currently the United Nations High Commissioner for Refugees, warns that "prevention is not, however, a substitute for asylum; the right to seek and enjoy asylum, therefore, must continue to be upheld."[6] Bill Frelick, a policy analyst for the U.S. Committee for Refugees, claims that the trend towards preventing refugee flows will endanger the most fundamental principles of refugee protection—the right of refugees to flee their countries and seek asylum from persecution. A strong advocate of the refugees' right to flee, Frelick recognizes that refugees are people willing to take extraordinary risks but says, "It is not up to us on the outside to limit their options and to make escape more difficult." Although the causes of flight most certainly must be addressed, he sees the need "to be able to offer immediate help to the Haitian who jumps on a boat and asks us for asylum or the Bosnian pleading to be allowed to cross to safety."[7]

Still others believe that because the numbers who want to move far exceed the capacity of host nations to receive them, these nations must reduce the number of refugees they accept and tighten restrictions on refugee policy. The many immigrants who enter the country illegally and then apply for asylum threaten the efficacy of a system designed to provide protection for a limited number of refugees. Citing the need for reform, the Center for Immigration Studies claims that:

> The orderly program for receiving refugees is not so orderly any more. Moreover, the escalation of admissions raises questions about whether there are in effect any real limits to this humanitarian immigration flow, or if the admissions will be constantly driven upward as long as world conditions continue to produce millions of additional refugees.[8]

Proponents of refugee policy reform often stress that not only is space in a host country limited but helping people who remain in their homelands is more cost efficient than allowing

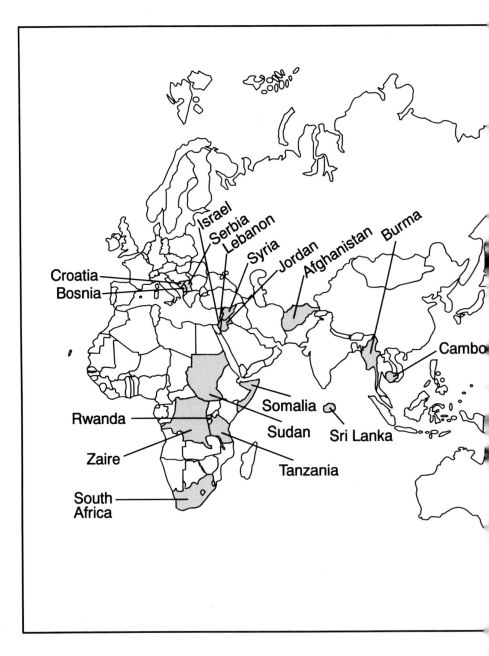

This map of the world highlights only those major areas of refugee flow which at discussed in this book.

United States

Cuba

Haiti

Guatemala

El
Salvador

Nicaragua

them to resettle. The Federation for American Immigration Reform has written:

> Many more refugees can be aided by financial support through the United Nations High Commission on Refugees (UNHCR) than by permanent resettlement in a country like the United States. The cost of helping refugees in UN-sponsored facilities is about six cents per day, while federal and state resettlement assistance for those who come to the U.S. to live permanently is about $6 a day. [9]

The international community must also face another obstacle—the issue of sovereignty, or the supreme power of a nation over its people. At what point should the international community intervene in the affairs of another country? Are the United Nations and other organizations morally obligated to provide assistance and protection to a people whose government may oppose such action? When and under what circumstances should a nation's sovereignty be undermined? These are questions that must be asked in an attempt to formulate refugee policy.

In 1970, the UNHCR estimated the number of refugees worldwide to be 2.5 million. By 1993, the number had multiplied eightfold. In Africa, 5.4 million people have had to abandon their homeland, and in Asia the number has risen to 7.2 million. Over 4 million of the world's refugees, including 2.9 million Afghans and 1.2 million Iraqi Kurds and Shiite Muslims, have found asylum in Iran. Pakistan has taken in 1.6 million Afghans, and Malawi provided asylum to 1 million from Mozambique.[10] These numbers serve to illustrate the severity of the refugee crisis and provide a stirring call to action.

Another increasingly large group of people who must abandon their homes do not cross an international border. Brutality, civil war, or famine have forced them to become homeless within their own countries. By a United Nations estimate, the number of the "internally displaced," as they are called, has reached 24 million. They can be found in Bosnia-Herzegovina, in the Sudan, in Haiti, and in Sri Lanka. Since they have not left their homelands, they cannot be recognized as refugees and therefore are not granted the same rights under international law. Nevertheless, the startling numbers of internally displaced have made an impact on the international community. Efforts to protect the rights of the internally displaced and end the strife that rendered them homeless are now underway.

The next chapter will trace the history of refugee movements in this century. The third chapter will describe organizations that protect the rights of refugees and help them integrate into a new society. Special attention will be given to women and children refugees, for they are the ones hardest hit by flight. Children, who represent one half of the refugee population, have often lost years of education and find it difficult to adjust. Many suffer from malnutrition. The lack of immunization causes serious illness and all too frequently premature death.

Subsequent chapters will examine the lives of refugees in different regions of the world. Refugees face formidable obstacles as they search for acceptance in a new land. They frequently encounter difficulties in receiving an education, preserving their cultural identity, and finding employment, without which they can secure neither food nor shelter. These problems will be discussed, as will those of the host countries already burdened with overpopulation, weak economies, and declining job markets. What options are open to a host country already wrestling with a situation defined by too many people and too few jobs?

Finally, the book will touch on what we, as part of an international community, can do to safeguard an individual's right to refuge, to protect the internally displaced, and to promote fair procedures for accepting refugees into host countries without giving those countries a burden too heavy to bear. It will also discuss potential solutions to avert refugee crises—promoting nonviolent resolution of internal conflicts through mediation or democratic elections, increasing funding for food, medical supplies, and literacy training, and preventing human rights abuses. We will see that only through greater protection of human rights can we create an environment in which a government does not force its people to flee their homeland.

The last chapter will serve as a reminder that studying the problems of refugees is not an answer. It is only a first step.

Refugees in History

History books have always recounted the stories of battles fought and won, of kings and conquered lands, of railroad empires and technological advances. They have told of generals, dictators, and presidents but often have neglected the people who sometimes suffered at their hands. In an attempt to change the way we view the past, many historians are now recounting the lives of those who were once victims of oppression but have been made strong by a combination of moral conviction and great courage.

The first historical reference to refugees is of a people persecuted for religious faith. Long before the modern era, individuals who held beliefs different from those of the majority often found that their rights were taken away. Some were tortured; many were forced into slavery; and still others were killed in religious wars. The lucky ones managed to escape. Hebrews in ancient history, the Jews and Moors in fifteenth-century Spain, the Huguenots in France, and the Puritans and Quakers in England all fled their native lands in search of a new home where they could freely practice their religions. Others, such as the Native Americans, became refugees when their land was taken away. In the twentieth century, world wars, political coups, and revolutions led to mass migrations of refugees.

War and Revolution

Air bombings and the use of poisonous chemicals and armored tanks helped make World War I the bloodiest war in the history of the human race. Over 10 million people died and twice that many were wounded. In addition, half a million soldiers were taken as prisoners of war, and many more found themselves as refugees without a home. The largest number, the Armenians—1,750,000 people—were forced out of Turkey into Syria and Palestine. Of this number, 600,000 died from starvation or were killed on their journey across the desert.

At the end of World War I, many countries joined together to form the League of Nations in an effort to maintain peace and to promote the international arbitration of disputes. In 1921, the League of Nations appointed Fridtjof Nansen High Commissioner for Refugees. The Norwegian statesman had previously worked as a zoologist and marine biologist. He had been the first to lead an expedition across Greenland and had also made a three-year trek to the Arctic.

After World War I, Nansen assisted in the return of the

prisoners of war and coordinated relief efforts for the refugees. He also provided refugees with internationally recognized identity papers to help them obtain legal rights. These travel documents, nicknamed "Nansen passports," eased the way for numerous refugees to return to their countries or seek asylum.

The Russian Revolution of 1917 and its aftermath caused the flight of 1.5 million people who tried to escape the new communist regime. A terrible famine in the winter of 1921 left even greater numbers of displaced people. To bring relief to the Russians, Nansen coordinated efforts for the League of Nations as well as the International Committee of the Red Cross, an organization founded in 1863 in Switzerland with the purpose of aiding war victims.

In 1921, Turkey and Greece engaged in a war that drove considerable numbers of Greek nationals out of Turkey. Nansen arranged for a population exchange controlled by the League of Nations: Two million Greeks left Asia Minor to resettle in Greece, and 800,000 Turks and 80,000 Bulgarians moved from Greece back to their countries of origin. The League compensated all those who took part in the eight-year resettlement plan.

India, after several attempts at self-government, received her independence from Great Britain in 1947. The divisiveness between Hindus and Muslims, however, did not allow for a smooth transition. Mahomed Ali Jinnah, leader of the Muslim League, demanded the creation of a separate Muslim state. Two separate nations were formed—India, which included most of the Hindu population and was led by Prime

Minister Jawarharlal Nehru, and, to the northeast and west, the mostly Muslim Pakistan, under Governor General Jinnah. This situation led to the oppression of the Muslims in India and of the Hindus in Pakistan. Both groups, as many as 8 million on each side, tried to flee from one country to the other, but many—200,000—were killed en route. Although it had first appeared that artful diplomacy would result in a peaceful changeover, in actuality, the new independence of both countries took its toll in human suffering.

World War II and the Holocaust

The horrors of the Holocaust began with Adolf Hitler's rise to power in Germany, the suppression of freedom of the press, the boycotting of Jewish goods, and the passage of anti-Semitic laws. Of the half million Jews living in Germany at the beginning of Hitler's dictatorship, 150,000 fled to Palestine, other parts of Europe, and the United States. After the night of November 9, 1938, known as Kristallnacht or "Night of the Broken Glass," when the Nazis attacked Jewish businesses and homes, breaking windows, burning buildings, killing 91 Jews, and arresting 30,000, still more attempted escape. But most Jews found it difficult to obtain a visa and were often barred entry into another country due to strict quotas that set limits on the number of immigrants. The Nazis drove the Jews out of their homes, took away their jobs, and moved them into cramped quarters in restricted areas called ghettos. Barbed wire or wooden fences separated them from other parts of the city. By 1941, the Jews had learned

After Kristallnacht, many Jews escaped to Shanghai, China, where they tried to reestablish their social, cultural, and religious institutions. They are shown here at a Friday night dinner in 1941.

that the ghetto was only a temporary way station. The Nazis would soon enter the ghetto and send the Jews in large groups to forced labor camps or concentration camps where millions would be put to death. Sometimes they would kill them on the spot.

On January 20, 1942, Nazi leaders met to plan what they called the "Final Solution"—the complete annihilation of the Jews. In desperation, Jews tried to find a refuge. Some made it to Spain or Portugal (which remained neutral during the war), and many fled across the English channel into Britain. Still others managed to reach the United States or Canada. Many hid in Nazi-occupied territory—Denmark, Holland, Belgium, the French Pyrenees.

Throughout Europe, Jews and non-Jews used cunning and courage to rebel against the Nazis. Witnesses to Nazi atrocities organized an underground movement called the Resistance. They provided false papers for Jews and published flyers urging people not to inform on the Jews. Raoul Wallenberg, a Swedish diplomat, traveled to Budapest where he provided Hungarian Jews with Swedish passports, which provided them with a measure of protection.

Jewish parents often made arrangements to send children into hiding. They hoped their children would survive the war; most knew they themselves did not stand a chance. It was more likely for a Jewish child to be mistaken for a Gentile than for an adult to escape recognition. Some were sent to live in convents, others were taken in by "a friend of a friend." They lived in attic rooms, secret hideaways, or cellars, often confined to the inside, never permitted outdoors. The lucky ones had windows. They had to remain silent and were not allowed to talk, laugh, or cry. The few times they went outside, they were taught to lie. Rosette Adler, a Holocaust survivor, recalls escaping by train with a neighbor, "I remember being told to say that he was my father. This was very difficult for me, because I was about three and a half."[1] The ones who survived grew old quickly—"The Nazis robbed them of their childhoods."[2]

The Holocaust resulted in the murder of over 6 million Jews, in addition to Gypsies, homosexuals, and other "undesirables." The Holocaust changed inexorably the religious composition of Europe, its culture, and its heritage. In Jerusalem, there stands a memorial to the Jews who died, called the Yad Vashem; it is a memorial also to those who survived and to those who risked their lives to help the refugees. Near the building is the Avenue of the Righteous, a path lined with carob trees. Each tree bears the name of a person who helped rescue a Jew. Since 1962, there have been 9,000 rescuers awarded a bronze medal on which are inscribed these words, "Whoever saves a single life is as one who has saved an entire world."[3]

The number of deaths brought about by World War II is staggering, impossible to comprehend. By the end of the war, 25 million civilians had died. The war's impact was felt around the world—millions were wounded; loved ones were lost; and, in Japan, those who had survived the atomic bomb had to contend with the lasting effects of radiation. In addition,

Two Jewish refugees, a sister and brother, arrive in Palestine in July 1944. They came from Romania where they had worked in peat pits after losing their parents.

the war had displaced 21 million people, leaving them without homes.

For years the ones who had escaped as children were rendered speechless by their inexplicable fate—why had they survived and others not? In 1991, the Anti-Defamation League of B'nai B'rith organized the First International Gathering of Children Hidden During World War II in New York City. The 1,600 in attendance gave voice to a common history. Each was once a refugee and was now still haunted by memories of family and friends who had not survived. Each one had a story to tell—of loneliness, courage, and victory over incredible odds.[4]

Their stories show us that we must look at the present with open eyes so that we may see the oppressed as well as the oppressor, the victim as well as the conqueror, the refugee as well as the violator of human rights.

Protecting the Refugees

Reacting to the horror of World War II, representatives from fifty nations met in San Francisco from April 25 to June 26, 1945, to found the United Nations, an international organization to encourage peaceful relations between countries. A new body was then established within the United Nations to oversee the protection of refugees, the International Refugee Organization. This organization helped with the repatriation and resettlement of the 21 million people who had been forced to leave their homes during the war.

Government-Sponsored Organizations

In 1950, the General Assembly of the United Nations resolved to replace the International Refugee Organization with the Office of the United Nations High Commissioner for Refugees. It defined its mission as "providing international protection and seeking permanent solutions for the problem of refugees."[1] The following year, the UN members agreed to the "Convention Relating to the Status of Refugees," a legally binding treaty that both defined the term "refugee" and outlined the principles of refugee protection and the rights of refugees. The word "refugee" first referred to a person living outside his or her former home country due to a "well-founded fear of persecution" for reasons of race, religion, nationality, membership in a particular social group, or political opinion. The convention also upheld the principle of "non-refoulement," which guarantees the right of a person not to be returned to a territory where he or she might be persecuted.

The original convention applied to Europeans who were displaced before January 1, 1951. It soon became apparent that other refugee groups were also in need of protection. A new "protocol," or agreement, issued by the United Nations in 1967, expanded the definition to include persons from outside Europe, as well as those who became displaced after 1951. Both the convention and the protocol have been signed by 111 nations.

The Organization of African Unity, composed of heads of state of most African nations, found that many people were forced to leave their countries not only as a result of persecution but also "owing to external aggression, occupation, foreign domination or events seriously disturbing public order."[2] In 1969, this organization drew up a "Convention

Governing the Specific Aspects of Refugee Problems in Africa," to help assure international protection for them.

In 1984, Central American nations also attempted to broaden the definition of refugee. They issued the Cartagena Declaration on Refugees to address the needs of those compelled to leave a country because their human rights have been violated. The Organization of African Unity convention and the Cartagena declaration illustrate the difficulties in defining the term "refugee." Under what circumstances should a person be guaranteed international protection? At what point can the United Nations High Commissioner for Refugees (UNHCR) intervene in the lives of people who are threatened by persecution, external aggression, or a violation of human rights? Must a person cross an international border in order to receive protection? These are a few of the questions that the UNHCR and other international organizations ask.

The General Assembly of the United Nations elects the UN High Commissioner for Refugees. This officer works to protect refugees and to promote "durable" solutions to their problems. The high commissioner must report to the executive committee, a body composed of representatives from forty-six governments that have a special interest in refugee problems. This committee oversees the funds used to protect and assist refugees. The UNHCR also coordinates the activities of 177 field offices, which are located around the world in 106 countries.

The high commissioner encourages governments to subscribe to international and regional conventions concerning refugees and promotes the granting of asylum to refugees. Other functions include ensuring that applications for asylum are examined fairly and that asylum-seekers are protected while their requests are being examined. The UNHCR works to provide refugees with the same economic and social rights as nationals of the country in which they have been granted asylum.[3]

The UN secretary-general, however, asked Sadako Ogata, who was named high commissioner in 1991, not only to fill the traditional role of protecting refugees who have left their home countries, but, in addition, to offer relief aid to refugees. In the past, the country that granted asylum supplied this aid. But now, since so many refugees are seeking asylum in less-developed countries, the UNHCR was asked to help provide food, shelter, medical aid, and educational opportunities. Sadako Ogata did not confine UNHCR assistance to refugees forced to leave their country; she also aided those living in refugee-like situations within their countries of origin. Since November 1991, for example, the UNHCR has overseen humanitarian aid to the 2.3 million war victims in Bosnia-Herzegovina.

International Red Cross

The International Committee of the Red Cross, an organization based in Geneva and supported by most governments around the world, visits and provides relief to prisoners of war and others in need of aid. Africa has received the largest proportion of aid from the Red Cross. (In 1992, the Red Cross brought 20,000 tons of food per month into Somalia and opened new orthopedic centers in Eritrea, Ethiopia, and Kenya.) The Red Cross also operates an information agency, called the Central Tracing Agency, for detainees and refugees. This agency coordinates family correspondence when this cannot be accomplished through regular means, traces missing persons, and issues travel documents to persons without identity papers. The use of computers has greatly facilitated much of the agency's work, including keeping records for 60 million people who have become displaced since 1914. (During the recent conflict in Bosnia, so many people were separated from family members that the Central Tracing Agency handled 20,000 messages a week.)[4]

The UN High Commissioner for Refugees and the International Committee of the Red Cross work in conjunction with many nongovernmental organizations to protect and assist refugees. These organizations provide refugees with tremendous resources and also serve as advocates for the refugees.

Private Organizations

The U.S. Committee for Refugees, a private organization based in Washington, D.C., which receives no government funds, sends emergency response teams to places where refugees need protection and assistance. After an on-site visit, they report on the conditions faced by refugees and displaced persons in hopes of receiving an effective response from the

Refugees from a Laotian hill tribe living in Chiang Kham camp in Thailand.

international community. In one year, teams may make assessments in as many as twenty-eight countries.

Refugees International, another private organization operating out of Washington, D.C., provides immediate on-site assessments of emergency situations. When the organization first hears of a crisis, it sends an emergency assessment team to the area. The team makes observations, consults with host-country representatives and government officials, and reports to local and international media. After the team leaves the affected area, Refugees International continues to act as an advocate—preparing newspaper articles and television appearances, briefing government and international organization officials, influencing policy makers, and delivering testimony to the U.S. Congress. In the past, Refugees International put pressure on Malaysia to stop turning away thousands of boat refugees from Vietnam, publicized the plight of Hmong refugees forced to return from Thailand to Laos, exposed the oppression of Cambodian refugees by the Khmer Rouge, and conducted emergency assessments and testified to Congress on the famine disaster in Africa.

Localized Refugee Assistance

Each group of refugees encounters specific problems stemming from cultural identity, causes for flight, or reception in the host country. Some problems, however, have proven universal. When refugees seek asylum, they invariably face obstacles in finding employment and securing an education for their children. The lack of language skills makes

A Cambodian refugee attends an ESL (English as a Second Language) class at Bunker Hill Community College in Boston.

it difficult to find a job. Without a means of employment, refugees can afford neither food nor shelter. Refugees become dependent on the host government or humanitarian agencies for the necessities of life.

Although the refugee resettlement process is most often handled by the federal government or private agencies, some U.S. states also play an important role. In Iowa, a state refugee bureau acts as a resettlement agency, service provider, welfare office, and employment agency. Oregon provides job training and English language programs. Refugees must participate in order to receive assistance checks. The city of Arlington, Virginia, has produced videotapes in different languages to ease the transition to a new culture; it has also organized apartment-based centers for language and job training and has arranged for local hotels to give release time to their employees so they can take language classes.[5]

Meeting the Needs of Women and Children

The refugees in greatest distress are most often the women and children. They suffer from poverty and malnutrition, which contribute to poor health. Women uprooted from their homes frequently become victims of violence and crime. They find that rape, abduction, torture, and forced prostitution are not uncommon. These abuses often precipitate the flight of refugee women from their home country. Burmese Muslim women who fled to Bangladesh told of widespread rape by Burmese government officials.[6] Serbian soldiers have also been accused of widespread rape in Bosnia. Escape to a refugee camp, however, does not necessarily assure safety. Harassment and violence have been reported in camps in Central America and Africa.

In war-torn areas, fathers are often absent. They may be fighting, wounded, or captured. Many have been killed. The disruption of normal family life and the separation from family members are difficult for children to overcome. They are left emotionally traumatized.

A great number of children, including those from Lebanon, Palestinian refugee camps, Mozambique, El Salvador, Sri Lanka, and Cambodia, do not attend school on a daily basis. They lose not only educational benefits but also a chance to see friends and receive health services, such as immunizations, which are often provided by schools. Many are pressed into military service and must risk their lives to fight alongside adults. An estimated 200,000 children (from eight to seventeen years old) now serve as soldiers in Afghanistan, Angola, Burma, Cambodia, El Salvador, Ethiopia, Guatemala, Honduras, Iran, Iraq, the West Bank and Gaza, Lebanon, Mozambique, Nicaragua, Peru, the Philippines, Sri Lanka, Sudan, Uganda, and Northern Ireland.[7] Many are refugees before they become soldiers. Others leave the military to find their homes destroyed, their families dispersed; they too have become refugees.

The UNHCR has worked to prevent abuses of women and children, to further educational opportunities for children, and to improve health care. It has sponsored school projects, which have been attended by an estimated 36 percent of primary school-age refugee children. Programs for secondary school students, however, have only reached 10 percent of refugee children in that age group.[8]

Other nongovernmental organizations have addressed specific problems faced by women and children. Save the Children, an organization founded in 1932, set up programs in Somalia, Sudan, Pakistan, and Zimbabwe to deal with the education and mental health needs of children, many of them refugees. In Thailand and Indonesia, it has placed an emphasis on literacy training, and primary and secondary education. Refugee Women in Development, based in Washington, D.C., trains women refugees in leadership development, as well as domestic violence prevention and intervention.

The International Rescue Committee, founded in 1933 by Albert Einstein to help the Jews escape persecution in Germany, continues to assist refugees. In recent years, it has been active in Asia, Africa, Central America, and Europe. In 1989, the Women's Commission for Refugee Women was started under the auspices of the International Rescue Committee to act as an advocate for women and children refugees. Fact-finding delegations testify before Congress and report to the U.S. State Department, UN officials, and other governments.

In September 1990, world leaders, including seventy-one presidents and prime ministers, met at the United Nations in New York for the World Summit for Children. They considered specific objectives to help promote the health and welfare of children. An agreement listing "year 2000 goals" has now been signed by 159 countries. These goals will have a significant impact on developing nations that have large refugee populations. Several of them are listed below:

- a halving of maternal mortality rates
- safe water and sanitation
- basic education and completion of primary education by at least 80 percent of the country's population
- a halving of the adult illiteracy rate
- the achievement of equal education opportunities for males and females
- family-planning education and prenatal care for women
- a one-third reduction in iron deficiency anemia among women and virtual elimination of vitamin A and iodine deficiency
- support of women in exclusive breastfeeding for the first four to six months of a child's life
- a halving of severe and moderate malnutrition among the world's under-five children
- the eradication of polio, neonatal tetanus, and guinea worm disease
- a 90 percent reduction in measles cases
- a halving of child deaths caused by diarrhea [9]

Many refugee children suffer from disease, famine, and lack of sanitation in their homelands, only to escape to a country that also has its share of health problems. Refugee workers and world health care organizations are working together to assure that the needs of refugees can be met.

Another vital mission of the United Nations Children's Fund (UNICEF) and others involved in the fight for the protection of children is the acceptance and observance of the Convention on the Rights of the Child.[10] This convention seeks to protect children in armed conflicts and to proclaim the right of all children to basic health care, nutrition, and education. The impact on children of refugees and the displaced could be enormous. The convention has now been ratified by 150 governments. Some progress has already been made in terms of protecting children in times of war. For example, during the recent conflict in El Salvador, "days of tranquillity" were established to allow for the immunization of children.

Many of the problems refugees confront daily in resettlement are connected to issues the world faces in providing food and health care for its people. A sustainable future for all men and women cannot be achieved until basic needs are met. UNICEF underlines the importance of alleviating poverty:

> It is clearly now possible to make a major impact by renewing efforts to overcome the worst aspects of the poverty that provides much of the impetus for both population growth and environmental stress in the developing world. Reducing child deaths, controlling malnutrition and disease, increasing family food production, and making family planning available to

all are ways of jump-starting a solution to many of these seemingly intractable problems. And achieving the basic human goals that have been agreed by the majority of the world's political leaders could therefore be considered a first test of the international community's willingness and capacity to begin making the great transition.[11]

Problems cannot be successfully treated in isolation; instead the international community—governments and non-governmental organizations—must work together to overcome the many burdens associated with poverty. The impact of a worldwide commitment to meeting basic food and health care would shake the world; its impact on the refugee population would be tremendous.

4

Refugees
in Latin America
and the Caribbean

Violence and human rights abuses in Peru, drug wars in Columbia, and political unrest in Haiti and Cuba have forced many people to leave their homes. Some have succeeded in leaving their countries; others have not been so successful. On the other hand, international mediation has led to repatriation—the voluntary return of refugees—in a few Central American countries. In discussing refugees in several countries in this region, the lack of stability in this area will become clear.

El Salvador, Nicaragua, and Guatemala

In the 1980s, civil wars in El Salvador, Nicaragua, and Guatemala left 2 million people uprooted. Many abandoned rural homes for the city; some were placed in "model villages" under military control; still others fled to neighboring countries, Mexico, and the United States. Central American presidents, beginning a peace process in 1988, called on the UN to address the problems of refugees and the displaced.

As a result, the UN and seven regional governments sponsored the International Conference on Central American Refugees (CIREFCA) in Guatemala in May 1989. Representatives from countries all over the world, as well as various international organizations, held a heated debate, finally reaching a controversial "Plan of Action." This plan stressed the importance of national dialogue and reconciliation as well as the nondiscriminatory treatment of refugees. The international community—the UN, governments of developed nations, and private international organizations—all shared responsibility for implementing the plan.

Nicaraguan refugees, many of whom had fled to Costa Rica, started their return to Nicaragua following elections held in February 1990. Nicaraguans, who in the past had fought opposite each other, now found themselves living in the same communities. This situation led to increased tension and a renewal of fighting. As a stopgap measure, the UNHCR initiated "quick impact projects," designed to bring temporary relief until larger scale development could take place. These projects, now underway, necessitate a small investment and help involve the community. But the question remains—what happens next? Can the community become self-sufficient, or is a broader development strategy necessary?[1]

Over a half million people left El Salvador in the mid 1980s. Most of those who escaped to Mexico or the United States remained there, but many of those who fled only as far as Honduras returned home. At one point, 21,000 Salvadoran refugees were living in camps in Honduras; almost all returned to their homeland, and the camps are now closed. The returning refugees settled on abandoned land in El Salvador, but when previous landowners came back to their homes and found the land occupied by others, tension mounted. An easy resolution is not in sight.[2]

Refugees who fled to Mexico from Guatemala started negotiations in 1991 with the Guatemalan government to organize their return. Members of human rights organizations as well as the Catholic church and the UN High Commissioner for Refugees helped mediate the process. On January 20, 1993, after two years of negotiation, 2,500 of the 50,000 refugees crossed the border between Mexico and Guatemala. An agreement was reached that guaranteed the following:

- the return of the refugees would be voluntary

- they would be assured the right to free association and organization, freedom of movement, and access to land

- they would be exempt from military service for three years

- international mediation, monitoring, and verification of the terms of the agreement would be permitted[3]

Although this solution sounded promising, the process proved to be full of problems. Guatemala's civilian government agreed to the negotiations but was not able to prevent human rights violations by its military. The Guatemalan

Guatemalan refugees, who had fled to Mexico, return home.

Human Rights Commission recorded more than 1,200 human rights abuses from January through October 1992, including 427 extrajudicial executions, 25 disappearances, and 100 cases of torture.[4]

Major questions concerning the role of the international community face Central America today: At what point should the International Conference on Central American Refugees (CIREFCA) withdraw and allow individual governments to oversee the resettlement of the refugees? Will the gains that have been made through CIREFCA be lost if CIREFCA activities stop? How capable is CIREFCA of helping with the region's problems? (These include inadequate land for those who have been previously displaced, uncertainty over ownership, weak civil institutions, including labor unions and courts, and the need for national reconstruction plans to repair civil war damage.)[5]

Cuba

After Fidel Castro assumed power in Cuba in 1959, thousands of Cubans abandoned homes and jobs to start a new life abroad. What they left was a socialist dictatorship with strong ties to the Soviet Union; what they sought was asylum in the United States and the freedom a democracy affords. The United States, as part of its policy of opposing international communism, passed a law to facilitate immigration procedures and allow Cubans to qualify for status as permanent residents a year and a day after their arrival.

With the dissolution of the Soviet Union in 1991 came a decline in the economic stability of Cuba. The number of Cubans seeking refuge in the United States rose dramatically although the risks remained high. Those who were caught attempting to escape Cuba were often imprisoned for up to three years. Nevertheless, some succeeded in making the ninety-mile journey by boat or raft; others arrived by plane. Pilots of crop dusters and helicopters defected, and in December 1991, a Cuban pilot diverted a plane from a domestic route and landed in Miami. Fifty of the fifty-three passengers requested asylum in the United States.

In August 1994, Castro, in a sudden and dramatic reversal of position, encouraged Cubans to leave the country. The United States administration, adopting a new policy, stated that it would no longer give preferential treatment to Cuban refugees. They would be detained at Guantanamo, the United States naval base in Cuba, while their applications were reviewed. The United States agreed to grant 20,000 visas a year to Cubans if Cuba halted the exodus of boat people. Panama and Honduras announced that they would provide a safe haven for 15,000 refugees.

Yet, the many Cubans taken to Guantanamo fear the uncertainty that is their future. "We risked our lives to find freedom, not to become prisoners," [6] said Wualsin Romero, a man who has made three attempts to escape by raft. Twice he was caught and sent to prison. After the third attempt, the U.S. Coast Guard intercepted him and sent him to Guantanamo. There, he remained in a tented village out of touch with family and friends, but many miles from the land he hoped to reach.

The flood of refugees from Cuba and other nations has taken a heavy toll on the state of Florida. Because Florida serves as the port of entry for thirty countries in the Caribbean and Latin America, the economic demands placed on the state by refugees and immigrants far exceed those of most states. "Today's international problems become Florida's problems tomorrow," the former director of the Latin American and Caribbean Center at Florida International University in Miami, Mark B. Rosenberg, reports. "Our geography gives us a proximity and immediacy to foreign affairs that we cannot escape."[7]

Haiti

Cubans are not the only ones seeking entrance to Florida; Haitians as well have sought a safe refuge on Florida's shores. The Lawyers Committee for Human Rights reported that between the years of 1981 and 1990, the U.S. Coast Guard interdicted, or blocked the escape of, 24,000 Haitians. A military coup in Haiti in September 1991, which ousted Jean-Bertrand Aristide, the country's first democratically elected president, made the situation worse by increasing the number of Haitians who attempted to flee.

The Coast Guard intercepted boats filled with Haitian refugees and took the passengers to the United States naval base at Guantanamo Bay in Cuba to be interviewed. Of the 34,841 persons held and questioned during the eight months

This political cartoon, which appeared in the *Chicago Tribune* at the time of the Haitian refugee crisis, suggests that the pilgrims would never have been allowed to land in America during President George Bush's administration.

following the coup, 11,262 were found to have a "credible fear of persecution." In May 1992, however, President George Bush ordered the Coast Guard to return all interdicted Haitians to Haiti. Further claims for asylum would not be heard. Bill Clinton, running for president, made a campaign promise to rescind President Bush's executive order, but, once elected, opted instead to continue the forced return policy. In June 1993, the U.S. Supreme Court upheld the constitutionality of the forced repatriation.[8]

The United States administration contended that most Haitians who attempted to escape were not refugees but economic migrants. Although their economic situation was desperate, they were not subject to persecution and therefore should not be allowed entry. They maintained that Haitians should not be encouraged to flee and risk their lives in unseaworthy boats.

Treatment of those who did manage to escape to the United States without being interdicted was controversial. Many believed that the government took far too lax a stance by allowing them to remain in the United States. The Carrying Capacity Network, an organization working to promote recognition of the relationship between population and environmental issues, reported:

> Even though the current approval rate for asylum is 20%, it is estimated that 80% of all asylum claimants permanently remain in the U.S. For growing numbers, U.S. asylum policy is a 'backdoor' immigration channel that provides a strong incentive to immigrate.[9]

The number of migrants who enter the country, apply for asylum, and spend years here waiting for the process to be completed creates a drain on resources designed for a more select group, those for whom refugee status has definitely been determined. David Simcox and Rosemary Jenks from the Center for Immigration Studies worry about the effects of this policy on the future: "Awareness abroad of the asylum system's lenience and ease of manipulation is a powerful incentive to thousands of other hopeful migrants abroad to try their luck."[10]

Carrying Capacity Network also pointed to the tremendous costs involved in receiving the Haitians. Once again, the state and local government must "end up footing most of the bill," which severely strains "their capacities to provide and pay for essential public services such as education, social welfare, and criminal justice."[11] Studies have shown that refugees and those who seek asylum, many of whom arrive with little or no money, are more likely to receive welfare than other immigrants. Some worry about the consequences of increasing pressure on the welfare system. "We cannot provide a safety net for the world; we risk becoming a global welfare magnet if we try," said journalist Don Barnett in a *National Review* article.[12]

Organizations involved with refugees, however, among them the UNHCR, the U.S. Committee for Refugees, Amnesty International, Americas Watch, and the National Coalition for Haitian Refugees, all urged that those who sought safety outside Haiti not be forced to return. The U.S.

State Department reported that although the level of political violence declined after the period immediately following the military coup in 1991, human rights abuses, including killings by the security forces (outside the law), disappearances, beatings, and political interference with the judicial process, continued.[13]

Haitian refugees and their advocates believed that the United States administration policy went against the principle of "non-refoulement"—the right of refugees not to be returned to a country where they would be persecuted. They pointed to the fact that for decades, Cubans were granted asylum and welcomed "with open arms." However, in what many consider a discriminatory act, Haitians—who are people of color and not fleeing a Soviet-dominated state—were turned away. They wanted the United States to stand up to the military dictatorship in Haiti, support new sanctions against Haiti, and allow the refugees to seek asylum in this country.

Public pressure on the Clinton administration intensified as reports of human rights abuses in Haiti increased. In May 1994, following a twenty-six-day hunger strike by Randall Robinson, an activist and executive director of TransAfrica, a lobbying group for Africa and the Caribbean, the administration changed its policy. It began a process to allow those Haitians who were interdicted at sea to apply for asylum before being returned to Haiti.

Those who did not try their luck at sea but hoped to receive refugee status before attempting the journey met with what

Representative Kweisi Mfume, chairman of the Congressional Black Caucus, protests United States policy towards Haiti on Capitol Hill, March 23, 1994. Also present: Representative Maxine Waters from California, Jesse Jackson, Randall Robinson (founder of TransAfrica, lobbying group), and Representative John Conyers from Michigan. Randall Robinson staged a twenty-six-day fast to exert pressure on President Clinton to stop the forced return of Haitian refugees.

many would consider bureaucratic nightmares. Applicants needed to request an interview with the International Organization for Migration and the U.S. Immigration and Naturalization Service in Port-au-Prince, Haiti's capital. Due to postal and phone systems that did not operate smoothly, applicants almost invariably made several trips to these offices. The illiteracy rate (90 percent of the population) also contributed to the difficulties in completing the application. Many feared that the number of trips necessary to finish the process and the lengthy waiting period, often lasting several months, would increase the personal risks of persecution. In less than a year, from February 1992 to December 1992, 9,389 "cases" (representing 15,580 persons) had inquired about the process, but only a total of 61 cases (representing 136 persons) were admitted. Many were never granted interviews, and others were rejected.[14]

Haitians who wished to leave their country found themselves in a quagmire of the worst sort. The ones who sought asylum in the United States through available channels in Haiti's capital only encountered frustration and became stymied in the process. But the future of those who attempted to escape without the proper papers was no less promising. They were returned by United States authorities to Haiti where they faced persecution and sometimes brutal torture. There was no easy way out.

In the case of *Sale* v. *Haitian Centers Council*, heard before the Supreme Court, the Haitians' attorney, Harold Koh, of Yale Law School, testified that M. Bertrand (a pseudonym)

52

was forcibly returned to Haiti and then "driven off the boat with fire hoses." That night he was taken from his bed and beaten. "His left arm was fractured, and he fled into hiding." Koh argued that "the right we claim is not a right of entry. It's simply the right not to be returned to Haiti, a country where our clients face political persecution."[15]

Professor Koh, speaking against the forced return of the refugees, pointed out that the Haitians were intercepted 700 miles away from the United States. They were prevented from finding sanctuary not only in the United States but also on the 700 islands between the United States and Haiti. What he calls "a floating Berlin Wall" prevented Haitians from fleeing. "This is not a polite, bloodless process that is going on," he said.[16]

In an effort to restore democracy, stop human rights abuses, and to reduce the number of Haitians attempting to flee, the United States threatened to invade Haiti and rid the country of its military dictatorship. Two days before the scheduled invasion, President Clinton dispatched former President Jimmy Carter, former Chairman of the Joint Chiefs of Staff Colin L. Powell and Senator Sam Nunn of Georgia (chairman of the Senate Armed Services Committee) on a diplomatic mission to Haiti's capital, Port-au-Prince. There, they met with Lieutenant General Raoul Cedras who had seized power in the 1991 coup. On September 18, 1994, only minutes before an invasion would have occurred, the two parties reached an accord. Sixty-one planes carrying paratroopers from three United States air force bases, already in the air, were recalled as the announcement of an agreement was made. Cedras and his colleagues would step down as soon as the Haitian parliament passed an amnesty law (in effect granting them an official pardon), but no later than October 15, 1994, at which point Jean-Bertrand Aristide would resume the office of president.

In a speech to the UN General Assembly on October 4, 1994, Aristide stressed the need for infirmaries and rural health centers, reforestation, road-building, and an increase in the number of schools and teachers. (In a country of two million children, only 750,000 were enrolled in school in 1994.) Aristide proclaimed that no progress could occur without the people embracing reconciliation and justice, "so there will be no trace of violence or vengeance. . . . Weapons have to be silenced for us to have peace."[17] On October 15, 1994, Aristide arrived in Haiti after three years in exile. Haitians cheered, danced, and sang in the streets as they witnessed his return.

The situation in Haiti following the military coup underscored the plight of boat people everywhere—those trapped on the waters of the Caribbean and others around the world who have taken to the high seas. For none of them is this what Professor Koh termed "a polite, bloodless process."

5

African Turmoil

Famine, ethnic tension, and civil war have ravaged much of Africa. Refugees flee from one country to another, but the conditions in which they live improve little, if at all. In April 1994, war in Rwanda between the Hutus and the minority group called the Tutsis resulted in the slaughter of 500,000 Rwandans. In one twenty-four hour period, 250,000 people escaped across the border to refugee camps in Tanzania. The number of Tutsis fleeing persecution by the Hutu militia exceeded 400,000. Many arrived in camp with "severe machete wounds."[1] Hutus, fearing revenge from the Tutsi rebels, also fled the country. By July 1994, the number of Rwandans that had escaped to Zaire reached 1.5 million. Relief workers reported that entire villages stayed together as they settled in camps. One hundred forty-seven tons of food were needed each day to feed the people in only one refugee camp at Ngara, Tanzania.[2] The demand for food, water, and medical supplies was unprecedented.

The UN High Commissioner for Refugees organized an

airlift using United States, German, and British cargo planes to transport food and medical supplies to Zaire. However, an outbreak of cholera among the refugees caused the deaths of hundreds of thousands and underscored the desperate situation, the absence of clean water and the scarcity of relief. Rwandans, no longer safe in Zaire, wanted to return home, but feared a recurrence of violence. Now that the Tutsis had gained power, Hutus were anticipating a climate of revenge. But, threats of revenge proved to be unsubstantiated rumors and thousands made their way back to Rwanda.

Washington Post reporter Keith Richburg tells of one refugee, Donathe Ntegeyiminsi, who fled Rwanda for the town of Goma in Zaire. He walked across the border on "thickly calloused feet and deformed legs," but found no food and little water. The cholera epidemic was "turning the once scenic lakeside resort into a city of dead." Ntegeyiminsi wanted to return home. He had fled "because he thought he might be killed. He came back because he thought he might die."[3]

In the United States, early unwillingness to recognize the extent of the crisis and disagreement over the role this country should play led to delays in providing much needed relief. Although 2,350 American troops were dispatched to help provide humanitarian relief, many criticized the United States for not responding with a stronger sense of urgency. Others remained wary of sending greater numbers of American troops into a situation where the objectives were not more clearly defined.

Rwandan refugees have suffered through Africa's most

More than 250,000 refugees fled from Rwanda to Tanzania in one twenty-four hour period during April 1994.

violent conflict in recent times. Although other African countries may not have experienced this degree of bloodshed in
such a short period of time, their own problems have led to
widespread movements of refugees. This chapter will focus on
Somalia and the Sudan, two countries in which war and famine have resulted in catastrophic change.

Somalia

In Somalia, an East African country bordered by the Indian
Ocean on the east and by Ethiopia and Kenya on the west,
300,000 people died as a result of a three-year civil war that
began in 1989. Three million Somalis abandoned their homes
in search of food and safety; of these, one million have found
refuge in another country. One woman recalls the time when
her family owned thirty camels, fifty goats, twenty cows, and
a house, but fighting between clans changed everything:
"They burned the house, they took the animals, they killed
my husband, and my child and I went hungry."[4] Although a
cease-fire was declared in the spring of 1992, violence in the
capital, Mogadishu, continued, resulting in an average
wounding by gunfire of 200 to 300 people each week.[5] By
summer, 200 people a day were dying in Mogadishu from
malnutrition and famine.

The International Committee of the Red Cross, using
ships, planes, trucks, and helicopters, organized a food mission that brought supplies to 2 million people. The Red Cross
also set up 900 community kitchens to provide hot meals for
the hungry. Maintaining security created a problem; looting

of supplies and vehicles was rampant. In August 1992, President George Bush ordered the United States military to airlift food into Somalia. The UN Security Council sent a force of 500 peacekeeping troops to help assure the delivery of the food, but they proved ineffective in quelling the violence and vandalism. From 50 to 80 percent of all food relief was stolen. The U.S. Center for Disease Control reported that Somalia's death rate was "among the highest ever documented" among civilians affected by famine. In December 1992, President Bush, with the approval of the UN Security Council, sent 20,000 troops to Somalia to ensure the delivery of the relief supplies.[6]

After fifteen months in Somalia, American troops departed in March 1994. Some say the military intervention prevented the decimation of the population by protecting the delivery of relief supplies. Others contend that the American government failed in its mission: No form of democratic government replaced the dictatorship of Mohammed Siad Barre who was overthrown in early 1991. Instead, Mohammed Farah Aideed, leader of one of the rebel groups, gained power despite initial opposition from the United States and the United Nations. Although factionalism existed within Aideed's own clan, it appeared that Aideed had enough backing to take charge.

Somali refugees, in a desperate attempt to escape the fighting, fled to Ethiopia and to Kenya. A UNHCR report tells the story of what life at a refugee processing center on a neutral strip of land was like. On the night of September 27,

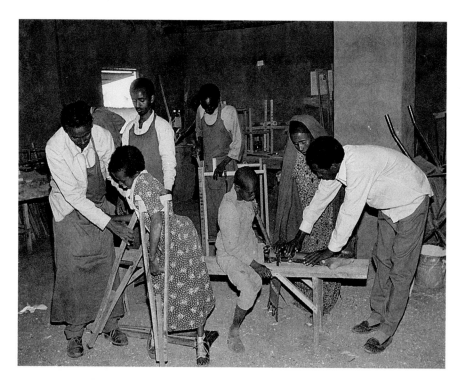

Somali refugees at an orthopedic center at the Hartisheik A camp in Ethiopia. Polio and accidents resulting from land mines are the cause of most disabilities.

1992, nearly 700 people arrived with hopes of registering as refugees. Many had walked a distance of 400 kilometers (250 miles) and were "dusty, footsore and exhausted."[7] The UNHCR team in charge of the screening process sent the ones most in need of medical attention to the hospital in the nearest refugee camp at Liboi. While the others waited for interviews, one family buried a three-year-old girl who died in the night, most probably from measles.

By early afternoon, 535 people were accepted into the refugee camp. Included in the group were three orphaned brothers in search of their uncle. The group boarded trucks for the ninety-kilometer (sixty-mile) journey to the camp. As soon as they arrived, relief workers issued ration cards to them and then took them to a distribution center run by CARE. First they acquired non-food items—a tent, blankets, a small stove, and water containers. After waiting in another line, they received flour, beans, oil, sugar, salt, and a tin of fish. Volunteers from the French organization, Médecins sans Frontières (Doctors Without Borders), gave each of the children a cup of milk, vitamin A, and a measles vaccine.

By nightfall, the refugees would have set up camp, found enough wood to build a fire, and cooked a meal. "The first day as a refugee is untypical, but it introduces some of the central elements of camp life: boredom, bureaucracy and endless standing in line," the report concludes. "The routine is like the diet: strange, distasteful and monotonous, but it is enough to sustain life and, perhaps, hope."[8]

By the end of 1992, Somali refugees in Kenya numbered

Refugees from the Sudan prepare a meal at the Fugnido camp in Ethiopia.

285,000. Kenya also hosted refugees from Ethiopia and the Sudan, bringing the total refugee population to 400,000, with an average of 900 entering each day. The UNHCR initiated a "crossborder operation" to expand their assistance programs on the Somali side of the border and thus reduce the number of refugees entering Kenya. The high commissioner hoped that by rehabilitating schools and clinics and encouraging a return to self-sufficiency in agriculture and livestock, the crossborder operation would be both preventive and solution-oriented.[9]

Francis Deng, a policy analyst, was once a human rights officer to the UN and is now the representative of the secretary-general of the UN on internally displaced persons. He believes that "the fundamental challenge of the Somali situation" is "not only to address the mass starvation and displacement but to consider the causes of the crisis." The solution lies in restructuring society and restoring self-sustaining social order. Although reconstruction will involve a more democratic government, Deng writes, "the values and institutions of the clan system" must not become "irrelevant."[10]

Sudan

The Sudan, the largest country in Africa, has, like Somalia, suffered tragic loss of life and severe famine. A total of 263,000 refugees have fled, and the number of displaced persons is even higher. The country's military, composed mostly of the Muslim population in northern Sudan, conducted a ten-year civil war against the Sudan People's Liberation Army, composed of southern Sudanese (Christians or followers of tribal religions). While relief efforts were under way, both sides were accused of stopping the delivery of supplies.

Thousands of Sudanese fled from southern Sudan, where most of the fighting took place, to cities in northern Sudan. One woman, named Akub, escaping from a southern village to Khartoum, explained, "now that we are here in Khartoum, our lives are no easier because we live on a garbage dump under a burlap bag. We are always afraid soldiers will bulldoze our camp and we will be forced to move again."[11]

The Sudanese government tried to relocate the southern Sudanese who had fled to northern cities. Some cited the need to prevent overcrowding, and others described an effort to purge the cities of non-Muslims. The U.S. Committee for Refugees has reported that in 1992 the government troops removed, often at gunpoint, 500,000 people from the city of Khartoum, forcing them into desert camps outside the city. After Judy Mayotte, a representative of the Women's Commission for Refugee Women and Children, visited the camps, she wrote, "The sites to which they were transported and dumped have no facilities for food, shelter, water, medicine, or sanitation."[12] A State Department official has called the relocation to barren sites "a condemnation to death."[13]

Government troops also burned the villages of the Nuba, an ethnic group in central Sudan. Africa Watch, a human rights organization, warned that such a policy would lead to the complete eradication of Nuba culture. Although the need for aid increased, the Sudanese authorities continued to reject help, fearing that the aid would most benefit the opposition. Two local employees of the U.S. Agency for International Development were executed by government forces, and three relief workers and a journalist were killed by a faction of the Sudanese People's Liberation Army in September 1992. The UN General Assembly accused the government of human rights violations, including "summary executions, detentions without due process, forced displacement of persons, and torture."[14]

Francis Deng, himself a Sudanese, has stated that the problems of the displaced cannot be solved until peace comes to the Sudan. In order for this to be achieved, Deng believes, a third party is necessary to negotiate a compromise.[15] Sadako Ogata, the UN high commissioner for refugees, writes that too often those who make up the refugee population are "dealt with as abstractions. They are mouths to feed, bodies to shelter, unknown victims of persecution and violence." The peace process is a key to the solution, but "freedom from want" must be seen "as an essential partner of freedom from war."[16]

Judy Mayotte believes that a lasting peace cannot be achieved without the prevention of human rights abuses. The internally displaced will continue to be "brutalized" by the government, "unless the questions of the limits of sovereignty in the face of human rights abuses is addressed."[17] In other words, the autonomy of a nation must be challenged when human rights are violated. Upholding those rights rests with the international community.

All across Africa, one can see that ethnic fighting and civil war have displaced large segments of the population. Although the civil war in Mozambique, after sixteen years of fighting, ended in 1992 and a repatriation program began, well over one million remained refugees and thousands more continued to flee their country. The tens of thousands of land mines that were hidden throughout the land threatened the safety of the refugees who returned to settle on unoccupied land. The end of apartheid in South Africa in 1993 and the first democratic election open to people of all races resulted in the return of thousands of exiles, and yet those who returned put themselves at risk. For most refugees, as well as repatriates, survival remains a struggle.

The words of Lionel Rosenblatt, executive director of Refugees International, underline the importance of foreseeing a potential crisis and putting a stop to it before the consequences reach tragic proportions. In 1992, a severe drought put 18 million people in southern Africa at risk of famine. The corn crop, a regional staple, failed. Rosenblatt called for the United Nations to appoint a "super-coordinator" to oversee the efforts of donor governments and organizations. Writing in the *International Herald Tribune,* he stressed the importance of an early response:

> We must learn to respond to emergencies before there is a huge loss of life. Right now there is drought in southern Africa. If it becomes a famine, it is a sin on us all. If we wait for the dying children to reach our television screens, it will be too late.[18]

Unrest in the Middle East

The Middle East has one of the longest-running and still unresolved refugee crises in the world. In 1948, the Arab-Israeli war resulted in the flight of 750,000 Palestinians from their homes. Fourth-generation Palestinian refugees are now growing up in camps constructed by their great-grandfathers. Many "have known nothing other than the limbo of refugee life," the UNHCR reports. For them, "conflict is the central ordering principle of their lives."[1]

On November 29, 1947, the UN General Assembly, in an attempt to aid Jewish refugees who had survived the Holocaust, voted to partition Palestine into separate Jewish and Arab states. On May 14, 1948, a Jewish provisional government, headed by David Ben-Gurion, announced the formation of the state of Israel. Neighboring Arab nations refused to recognize Israel, and fighting broke out the next day. By May 1949, Israel had laid claim to 8,000 square miles of

the land mandated to Palestinians in the original UN partition. Of the thousands of Palestinian Arab refugees, many
found asylum in Persian Gulf states; others moved into the
neighboring Arab states, and some remained in the territories
occupied by Israel. In 1950, Jordan annexed land on the West
Bank of the Jordan River.

In the Six Day War, in June 1967, Israel seized the West
Bank from Jordan, the Gaza Strip (a narrow piece of land in
southwest Palestine) from the United Arab Republic, the Sinai
Peninsula from Egypt, and the Golan Heights from Syria,
thus increasing its territory threefold. Israel returned the Sinai
to Egypt in 1982 but still occupied the other territories. The
Palestine Liberation Organization (PLO) was organized to
represent the cause of the Palestinian Arabs; it sought to abol-
ish the state of Israel and recreate a Palestine state. The PLO,
which has used guerilla war tactics against Israel, was not offi-
cially recognized by the United States until 1993, when the
leaders from Israel and Palestine met to negotiate a peace settlement that would recognize the rights of both Israelis and
Palestinians.

The UN General Assembly organized the United Nations
Relief and Works Agency for Palestine Refugees in the Near
East in 1949. Initially, the UN gave the agency only the right
to provide relief but not to protect refugees or promote solutions to refugee problems. This meant the refugees had no
advocate for protection. In 1988, UN General Assembly reso-
lutions provided a limited degree of protection by allowing

Palestinian refugees in the Gaza Strip receive food parcels and milk powder from the United Nations Relief and Works Agency.

the agency to offer legal aid and increase international and local staff.

In 1986, Palestinians in refugee camps in the Gaza strip started sending out a new message. In an uprising that became known as the intifada,[2] they called for a two-state solution (Palestine and Israel); gone was the emphasis on eliminating the state of Israel. Palestinians in cities and towns later joined forces in protests that involved not tanks or machine guns, but clubs, kitchen knives, rocks, and bottles. The Israelis retaliated with limited gunfire, imprisonment, tear gas, plastic bullets, and a machine that could throw pebbles at high speeds. Israeli security forces, in the camps disguised as Arabs, made arrests that sometimes resulted in shooting and death. They also responded by demolishing houses, uprooting trees, and enforcing night curfews. In one year alone, from July 1991 through June 1992, the UN Relief and Works Agency reported treating 5,360 people for bullet wounds, beatings, and tear gas inhalation.[3]

Israeli security forces have often blocked the United Nations' attempts to assist the refugees. Schools have been closed and ambulances stopped. The U.S. Committee for Refugees reports that on March 9, 1992, a UN ambulance transporting a man shot during a disturbance in a camp in the West Bank was forced to wait ten minutes at the camp's entrance while security forces checked the driver's identification and searched the vehicle. The victim died before reaching the hospital.[4]

The number of Palestinian refugees living in Jordan, Syria, Lebanon, the West Bank, and Gaza has now reached

2.7 million. Jordan has received the highest number of refugees—as many as 1 million. This number includes the 180,000 Palestinians who fled to Jordan from Kuwait following the Iraqi invasion in 1990. Their arrival caused an immediate increase in the number of unemployed and also placed pressure on the educational and health care systems as well as the housing market. Jordanians found it difficult to meet the rising demands. Schools in refugee camps became overcrowded—most hold two sessions, morning and afternoon; many classes have sixty-five students in one room. A 1991 Jordanian Health Ministry study found a 34 percent increase in the number of people seeking health care.

An Oxford University study has found that refugee families in Jordan must spend 80 to 90 percent of their income on food. Their limited diet includes bread, tea, tomatoes, lentils, and onions. Green vegetables and fruits are hard to come by.[5]

Although the influx of refugees first created a boom in the construction business, it also resulted in overcrowded slums in the cities. Many refugees were forced into temporary housing—230,000 Palestinians now live in Jordan's ten refugee camps. The U.S. Committee for Refugees, reporting on a camp in Jerash in 1993, found that shelters, which had been constructed of asbestos and zinc sheets in 1967 and were expected to last only five years, were still in use but were falling apart. Houses meant for five people were accommodating fifteen. Open sewage channels led to an increase in parasitic diseases and infections.[6]

Before the Gulf War, which began with the Iraqi invasion

Many refugee camps in Lebanon were destroyed during the sixteen-year civil war.

of Kuwait, 320,000 Palestinians lived in Kuwait. After the war, the government attempted to purge the country of noncitizens. Palestinians who had fled were not allowed to return. Those who had remained lost their jobs; their children were not allowed to attend government schools. The U.S. Committee for Refugees also reported that Kuwaiti vigilante squads were responsible for torture and killings. By 1993, many had escaped, but 20,000 Palestinians still remained.[7]

A sixteen-year civil war in Lebanon resulted in the displacement of thousands of Palestinian families, much violence, and many human rights abuses. Thomas Friedman, a *New York Times* reporter who lived in Lebanon, points out that for a three-year period, from 1985 to 1988, Palestinians in Lebanese refugee camps were often the victims, not only of Israelis, but of other Arabs, and yet "it was almost always back page news—if it was reported at all. This despite the fact that some 3,000 Palestinians were killed during the three years of fighting over the camps, including women who were shot by snipers while going out to buy bread and others who died of hunger after having run out of dogs to eat."[8] The UN was able to provide emergency relief for 7,000 families in 1992, but educational opportunities have been especially limited due to the war. As a consequence, large numbers of refugees remain illiterate.

A program called Interns for Peace sends teams of young Jews and Arabs into towns in the Middle East to organize dialogues between Arab and Jewish children and help build relationships. Laura Blumenfeld, a Harvard student and president of the Zionist League, a Jewish nationalist organization, was preparing to host a dinner at the Harvard Hillel for the Arab Students' Society when she received a call from her father who was visiting Israel. He first told her, "Laura, I'm okay, no matter what you hear on television," and then explained that he had been the victim of a random bullet, fired by an Arab. Laura proceeded to the dinner a half hour later. She was shaken, but she came to the realization that she needed to do something more to bring Israelis and Arabs together. She would join Interns for Peace.[9]

Peace talks between Arabs and Israelis held in Washington, D.C., in April 1992 resulted in the formation of the Multilateral Working Group on Refugees. In November 1992, the group reconvened in Ottawa, Canada. Professor Shlomo Ben-Ami, chairman of the Israeli delegation, expressed concern for the refugees by calling their camps "an affront to human dignity and a moral burden on our collective conscience." He called for "the philosophy of welfare and relief" to give way to "rehabilitation." He also proposed a plan that would include new housing, improved sewage systems, road systems, street lights, telephone networks, playgrounds, youth clubs, and shopping centers. What was not discussed, however, was the issue of family reunification. The Israelis still refused to consider the right of the Palestinians to return to their homeland.[10]

On September 13, 1993, a momentous change took place. Yitzhak Rabin, prime minister of Israel, and Yasir Arafat, chairman of the PLO, met in Washington, D.C. with

President Bill Clinton to sign an agreement known as the Mideast Accord. Its goal was to create an interim Palestinian government to be run by an elected council that would serve for a maximum of five years, while negotiations would be carried out for a permanent Palestinian government within the West Bank and Gaza Strip. A special committee was to be established to decide on the repatriation of the 100,000 people displaced from the West Bank and Gaza Strip in 1967. In this historic meeting, Rabin announced:

> We have come from an anguished and grieving land. We have come from a people, a home, a family that has not known a single year, not a single month, in which mothers have not wept for their sons. . . . Let me say to you, the Palestinians . . . we are destined to live together on the same soil in the same land. . . . We say to you today, in a loud and a clear voice: enough of blood and tears. Enough.

Arafat called for international participation in the process and said, "Putting an end to their feelings of being wronged and of having suffered an historic injustice is the strongest guarantee to achieve coexistence and openness between our two peoples and future generations."[11]

Violence in the Middle East and human rights abuses have not ceased. Although many difficulties remain to be overcome, Rabin's and Arafat's words have laid the building blocks for a period of progress in Arab-Israeli relations. These words are the building blocks; the outcome remains in question.

chapter

7

Repatriation in Asia

In the early 1990s, Asian countries were host to the largest number of refugees in the world. Refugees fled from countries all across the continent—from Bhutan, a small country in the Himalayas undergoing ethnic tension; from Tajikistan, a country that declared its independence from the Soviet Union in 1991 and was then plagued by civil war; and from Tibet, where the Chinese government subjects followers of the Dalai Lama to human rights abuses. At the same time, Asians also witnessed the repatriation of refugees on a scale that was unprecedented. What follows is a discussion of repatriation in several countries—Afghanistan, Cambodia, Burma, and Sri Lanka. The problems these refugees faced when they returned to their homeland, either voluntarily or under coercion, will be examined.

Afghanistan

The Soviet invasion of Afghanistan in 1979 led to a fourteen-year war between the mujahedin (Afghan rebel groups supported by the United States) and the Afghan government troops (formerly backed by the Soviet Union). Three million Afghans fled to Iran and another 3.5 million to Pakistan, making Afghans the largest refugee population in the world.

One girl named Farida tells of arriving in Peshawar, a Pakistani town near the border, to find that girls were not allowed to attend school. Farida and her sisters "watched the males go to school, and we wanted to go, too. I feared if I ever did go to school again, I would be very old when I finished."[1] Her mother Tajwar dreamed of starting a secondary school for girls but only met with frustration. She bought a knitting machine and made clothes at home, which brought in one or two dollars a week, not enough to feed a family of ten. After two years of persistent negotiating on Tajwar's part, on March 1, 1987, the school, Lycee Malalai, opened its doors to girls.

At the Mohammed Kheil camp near Quetta in Pakistan, where refugees lived in tents, a group of women started a sewing group. In 1992, the group of 600 women produced 20,000 quilts. For the year's work, the entire group was paid 350,000 rupees, or $20,000, which came to $35 a year for each woman. When Judy Mayotte of the Women's Commission for Refugee Women and Children visited the camp on payday, she watched each woman put her thumb print in a

Afghan refugees in Munda village in the Peshawar region of Pakistan.

square next to her name as she received her pay. She realized then that none of the women could read or write.[2]

Latifa, an Afghan woman who came to Peshawar, found that she "was not prepared for the extent to which the fundamentalist Muslims had taken control of the life of the refugee community."[3] Latifa believed that fundamentalists often discouraged literacy and denied women job opportunities and equal rights in the name of religion. But there is no basis for this in the teachings of the prophet Mohammed or in the Koran, the Muslim sacred text. She and a friend, Sohaila, both Muslims, created the Afghan Women's Center, an institution run by and for Afghan women to help them understand women's relationship to Islam and to provide the poorest women with self-sufficiency skills. As they entered the center, women removed their veils and sat on floor mats for their lessons. Sohaila imparted to them her belief that:

> Without literacy a woman has no control over herself. If she is not literate, she will have no access to information. Without information, a woman cannot become a part of the decision-making process in the wider community. She will remain forever closed off to a greater part of the world.[4]

Ten years after the invasion, the Soviet occupation of Afghanistan ended. The Geneva Accords called for the repatriation of the refugees, but it was not until April 1992, when the mujahedin took over Kabul, the Afghan capital, and overthrew the government leader installed by the Soviets, that significant numbers started to return. A UNHCR program encouraged refugees to turn in their ration cards for an assistance package of 300 kilograms of wheat and 3,300 rupees ($130) to pay for transportation back to Afghanistan as well as a few necessities. By 1992, an overwhelming number of refugees—1.8 million—had repatriated.[5]

The proliferation of land mines has endangered the return of the refugees. It has been estimated that there are two mines for every Afghan, bringing the total number of land mines to 30 million. Groups from many countries continue to de-mine the land. The Royal Thai Government donated a dog team trained to detect mines. Each dog finds an average of five or six mines a day; some dogs can find as many as fifteen.[6]

Refugees continued to return, but fighting among various mujahedin factions did not cease. In August 1992, violence in the capital left between 1,000 and 2,000 dead and 9,000 injured. Half a million of the city's inhabitants fled. Unrest outside the capital also caused tens of thousands to become displaced. While many returned from camps in Pakistan, others took their places. The U.S. Committee for Refugees reports that more than 12,000 moved into "the ruins of refugee camps that repatriating refugees left behind."[7] The emphasis placed on repatriation by the international community has left many of the refugees still in Pakistan and Iran stranded. Security has decreased, schools are closed, and food is becoming scarce.

Cambodia

In 1991, after twenty years of war, Cambodia found itself in a state of turmoil. First had come American bombing during the Vietnam War. The communist Khmer Rouge regime, which repeatedly and harshly violated human rights—suppressing dissent and performing mass executions, followed in 1975. The invasion by Vietnam in 1978 put an end to many of the Khmer Rouge's cruel practices but led to the flight of 350,000 Khmer to camps along the Thai border. Most remained imprisoned behind barbed wire. Others were sent back at gunpoint to their country where Vietnamese forces awaited them.[8] For thirteen years, the Cambodians made unsuccessful attempts to overthrow the Vietnamese.

Judy Mayotte, visiting the Khmer in camps, found they had lost many of the traditions that made them a people. Humanitarian assistance was "similar to a Band-Aid over a lethal wound." What they needed, she said, was the opportunity to return home.[9]

On October 23, 1991, the Cambodian Peace Accords were signed in Paris. Nineteen nations participated in the making of what has been called "a fragile peace."[10] The accords provided "special measures to assure protection of human rights, and the non-return to the policies and practices of the past."[11] The various parties agreed that the UN Transitional Authority in Cambodia, a peacekeeping organization, would have control over the Vietnamese-installed government, the Khmer Rouge's party, and other factions. A Supreme National Council, including representatives of all factions, would be invested with some authority, but the UN Transitional Authority (UNTAC) would maintain the upper hand. It would oversee the cease-fire, the withdrawal of the

Vietnamese forces, and the clearing of millions of land mines. Article 14 of the peace accords made UNTAC responsible for ensuring human rights by providing education, investigating complaints, and taking corrective action.[12]

In the several months following the signing of the peace accords, the UNHCR devised a repatriation plan for the refugees.[13] On March 30, 1992, the UNHCR helped transport 525 refugees from Thailand into Cambodia. The UNHCR's first plan was to offer each refugee family two hectares (approximately five acres) of agricultural land in their choice of destination. However, the scarcity of available land that had been cleared of land mines prevented the UNHCR from fulfilling its promises.

A second plan offered refugees travel assistance, protection, and one of four forms of resettlement aid—two hectares of agricultural land (not necessarily in the province of choice), a small plot of land and building materials to construct a home, a cash allowance of $50 for each adult and $25 for each child, or technical assistance to start a small business. Each family also received a 400-day supply of food, household utensils, and agricultural tools.[14]

Land still proved difficult to come by, so the majority of refugees chose the cash allowance. Fighting in the western part of the country forced the people east. Boarding the Sisophon Express, they traveled by train from Thailand to Phnom Penh in southeastern Cambodia. This train made 71 trips and carried a total of 90,000 returnees.[15] The refugees headed first to the UNHCR reception center and from there

Cambodian refugees return from Thailand to Phnom Penh on the Sisophon Express, a train that made seventy-one journeys to transport 90,000 returnees.

made their way into neighboring districts with help from the Cambodian Red Cross. By March 1993, 349,000 Cambodian refugees had returned home. On March 30, the UNHCR closed its last Cambodian refugee camp in Thailand.[16]

Refugees were not the only ones left homeless by the war. One hundred eighty thousand people were displaced but never left the country. Abandoning their homes to escape the fighting, many had to accept poorer conditions among relatives or in camps. Beng Ampil, the largest camp for internally displaced, accommodated 12,000 displaced persons. Surrounding the camp was an area covered with land mines.

Francis Deng reports that international aid programs help the refugees who have returned but not the internally displaced who never crossed an international border. The UN Transitional Authority officials and nongovernmental organizations "recognized the disparities and sought to plan community-wide activities to benefit both refugees and displaced persons," he said. "The distinctions, however, have proved difficult to erase." He believes the Cambodian situation highlights the necessity for humanitarian assistance and resettlement plans "to reflect demonstrable needs rather than artificial geographic boundaries and labels."[17]

Burma and Sri Lanka

In other parts of Asia—Burma and Sri Lanka, for example—large numbers of refugees have been forced to flee and then coerced back to their homelands. In Burma and Sri Lanka, both of which suffer from the devastation of civil war, the UNHCR has encountered many difficulties in paving the way for refugees to return.

Burma lies south of China, nestled between India and Bangladesh on one side and Thailand on the other. By 1992, more than 330,000 Burmese had been driven out of the country by the military dictatorship of Burma. The vast majority of the refugees—245,000 Rohingyas, a Muslim people—fled to Bangladesh; others fled to Thailand, China, Malaysia, and India. In Bangladesh, the local residents claimed the large numbers of refugees were destroying their lands and forests. The government, therefore, tried to force the Rohingyas to return by reducing daily food rations, imposing burdensome regulations on relief groups, and restricting the movements of refugees in and out of camps.[18]

Refugees International reported that nighttime beatings have also occurred "to induce refugees to 'volunteer' to go home."[19] In October and November 1992, 167 of the 932 refugees who repatriated told the UNHCR they had not wanted to repatriate. In December, the UNHCR announced that it would refuse to participate in the repatriation program. Sadako Ogata, UN High Commissioner for Refugees, publicly called for the end to "coerced returns,"[20] but repatriation did not totally cease. Of the 6,000 repatriations that took place in 1992, only 900 were considered voluntary by the U.S. Committee for Refugees. In early 1993, the Bangladesh government finally agreed to allow the UNHCR to monitor the returns and stop forced repatriation.

Yet another human tragedy is unfolding in Sri Lanka, the

Refugees from Burma cross the Naf River into Bangladesh.

island country off the coast of India. In the 1980s, fighting between the Sinhalese (a Buddhist ethnic group that makes up three fourths of the population) and the Tamils (a Hindu minority group) led to an exodus of hundreds of thousands of refugees. Six hundred thousand people were uprooted, and thousands were killed or reported missing. A delegation from the UN Working Group on Enforced or Involuntary Disappearances reported 12,000 disappearances between 1983 and 1991.

Within a decade, a half million Tamils had fled, many crossing the Palk Strait into India, and others heading for parts of Europe. India welcomed the refugees until the assassination of the Indian prime minister, Rajiv Gandhi, by a suicide bomber, suspected of being of Tamil origin, in May 1991. This led the Indian government to reverse its position and require the Tamils to repatriate.

The number of Tamils who returned both voluntarily and involuntarily totalled 29,000 during 1992. The UNHCR established Open Relief Centers in Sri Lanka to help returnees and deter others from leaving. One Tamil left his home and went as far as the Open Relief Center at Madhu. "We came to Madhu so that we could go to India from here," he explained. "But then we heard that UNHCR had plans to establish a camp. We decided to remain here because we felt this camp gave us protection from the army attacks and aerial bombing that forced us to leave our homes."[21]

In the early 1990s, Asia provided the stage for the repatriation of more than 2 million refugees—both voluntary and

87

involuntary. The difficulties involved in the process are readily apparent: the lack of protection, the scarcity of jobs, the limited educational opportunities. The hardships returnees endure range from basic survival in a land strewn with mines, where food is insufficient, and human rights continue to be abused, to reintegration into a society from which they fled long ago.

The United Nations and nongovernmental organizations must exercise vigilance in stopping forced repatriations. Assistance needs to be given to countries that find the burden of accepting overwhelming numbers of refugees too much to bear. The international community must share the responsibility so that no one country shoulders more than it can handle.

The UNHCR and others constantly weigh how they can be most effective. Pulled in different directions, they face a difficult choice—to find a home for refugees outside the country of origin or, by changing the conditions that force people to flee, to facilitate their return.

chapter

8

Bosnian Tragedy

Ethnic tension, coupled with the sudden fall of communism in the former Soviet Union, has led to tremendous numbers of refugees fleeing newly independent nations. For two of these countries, Armenia and Azerbaijan, the rise of nationalism has given way to ethnic cleansing—or the removal of an ethnic minority from a country where the majority—and only the majority—rules. What is happening in this part of the world is reflected in the former country of Yugoslavia, where ethnic rivalries have resulted in civil war, human rights abuses, and the destruction of a richly diverse multiethnic culture.

Sarajevo, the capital of Bosnia, is a city that endured a 700-day siege by Serbs that came to a bitter end in March 1994. Here, people had to get by without water or electricity. Heavy shelling and exploding bullets often made it impossible to bring food and aid into the city.

As a result of ethnic cleansing, Bosnian children arrive at the Gasinci camp in Croatia.

Most of the relief that found its way into Sarajevo came from humanitarian organizations, but, on occasion, individuals ventured out on their own. Such was the case of American doctors from Virginia who traveled to Bosnia and received passes to enter as truck drivers, not as doctors, to avoid bureaucratic problems. One orthopedic surgeon, David Snyder, a Vietnam veteran, says he made the trip because of "unfinished business" in Vietnam. His experience there as a doctor made him feel compelled to offer his services in Bosnia. Having seen the tremendous need in a war-torn country, he knew he could help.

Another member of the group, Les Enterline, a physician's assistant, once a volunteer in a Haitian clinic, was taken to the morgue in Sarajevo where he saw the bodies of five children, killed by a mortar blast. Enterline thought of his own four young children and quoted a Haitian proverb, "The heart can't feel what the eyes don't see." He added, "The only difference between my children lying there and them is the country they were born in."[1]

Before the Balkan war, Bosnia contained a population rich in ethnic and religious diversity—44 percent Muslim, 31 percent Serb (Orthodox Christian), and 17 percent Croat (Roman Catholic). With the breakup of Yugoslavia, Serbs in both Bosnia and Serbia feared that they would lose their level of influence in an independent Bosnia that was mostly Muslim. In an effort to assert greater authority, they attacked the Muslims, killing civilians, raping women, and forcing hundreds of thousands of people from their homes. The attempt to rid the country of non-Serbs became known as ethnic cleansing. In 1993, the U.S. Committee for Refugees reported that Serb aggression had left 100,000 dead, 60,000 missing, and 740,000 displaced. The number of victims who fled Bosnia reached 1.1 million. [2]

Most Bosnians escaped to other republics of the former country of Yugoslavia—Croatia, Serbia, Slovenia, Montenegro, and Macedonia. Other European countries closed their doors to the Bosnians, claiming that if they took in refugees, they would be contributing to ethnic cleansing and abandoning Bosnia to the Serbs. The Yugoslav republics soon followed the example set by the rest of Europe and refused to accept refugees.

The United Nations and the European Community both participated in mediation efforts. Various parties reached agreements, but the written and spoken words appeared insignificant. A cease-fire would be agreed to, and then forgotten. Many promises were made, and many broken. Time after time, a plan for peace was in the offing, but never within reach.

In July 1992, the United Nations led a humanitarian airlift to Sarajevo. By the end of the year, twenty countries had taken part, bringing food and other relief supplies, sometimes as much as 200 metric tons per day. The UN protection force helped make it possible to fly supplies into Sarajevo. Limited aid went to Sarajevo, but little, if anything, reached those outside the capital. The U.S. Committee for Refugees reported that most of these people suffered "relentless bombardments" and were "forced to remain in cellars and eat roots to survive."[3]

Although most Muslims could not escape the Balkan war,

one woman, Zeyneba Hardaga, found refuge in Israel. During World War II, she had hidden a Jewish family from the Nazis in Sarajevo. In 1985, she visited Jerusalem where she received the Righteous Gentile Award, given to non-Jews who rescued Jews from the Nazis. Eight years later, during the siege of Sarajevo, she lived in a darkened room in a building that had been the site of a mortar attack that had killed five people. Now her turn to receive help had come. Tovah Grinberg, who was a three-year-old child when Zeyneba had provided protection for her family in Nazi Germany, made possible Zeyneba's escape to Israel.

"I feel like this is my family," Tovah said, as she greeted Zeyneba at the airport in Jerusalem on February 11, 1994. "When you are 76 years old, you need only a little love, peace and a normal life," Zeyneba's daughter, Aida, told *Washington Post* reporter David Hoffman. Aida, her husband, and daughter accompanied Zeyneba and are now among the 1,000 Bosnian refugees who have been granted asylum in Israel.[4]

The situation in Bosnia illustrates the problems the international community faces in dealing with a refugee crisis. The United States and European countries were often criticized for not using military force to control the Serbs and put an end to ethnic cleansing, considered by many a form of genocide. The atrocities perpetrated on the Muslims were so great that many maintained airstrikes were justified. Yet others thought the solution still lay in mediation. They sought a way to partition the land so that Serbs, Muslims, and Croats could each have a piece to claim as their own. Although the Vance-Owen

Bosnians find refuge on a football field of the Kuknic Sports Center in Rijeka, Croatia—the first tented camp in Europe since World War II.

talks (organized by Cyrus Vance, representing the United Nations, and Lord David Owen, representing the European Community) did not bring about a peaceful settlement, those believing in negotiation did not lose faith in the process. They believed the use of force would not only increase the human toll but do little to bring about a peaceful outcome.

For still others, the failure lay not with a choice poorly made but with a response that was both indifferent and weak. Bill Frelick of the U.S. Committee for Refugees states that:

> The world community stood by idly, neither providing protection against the onslaught, nor allowing the Muslims to defend themselves, while holding Bosnia to the arms embargo on all parts of former Yugoslavia, despite the clear disproportion of arms already in Serbian hands. . . . By keeping their arms folded and their doors shut, the United States and other governments suggested that the conflict was not of vital concern to their own interests, giving a green light to Serbian militias to continue their slaughter and to neighboring Croatia to close its border with Bosnia.[5]

Writing in defense of the U.S. administration, Nancy Soderberg of the National Security Council claimed that the United States did not stand idly by. "American leadership has made a difference in enforcing the sanctions and no-fly zones, sustaining the longest airlift in history, protecting U.N. forces with NATO air power, pressing for a war crimes tribunal and concluding the Muslim-Croat agreement."[6]

Zlata Filipovic, a young Bosnian girl whose wartime diary

A drawing by a thirteen-year-old Croatian shows the fighting between the Croatians and the Serbs. This picture belongs to a collection titled "Children's War Art from Bosnia and Croatia," which was exhibited in Washington, D.C., and other cities across the United States.

was published in 1994, shows that no one emerges from war unscathed, least of all the children. Before Zlata was allowed to leave Bosnia in December 1993, she spent much of her time hidden in her neighbor's cellar or kitchen. She tells what it was like not to have running water or electricity:

> We have an unusual way of bathing. We spread out the sheets of plastic and then—the basin becomes our bathtub, the jug our shower, and so on. Daddy's got frostbite on his fingers from cutting the wood in the cold cellar. They look awful. His fingers are swollen and now they're putting some cream on them, but they itch badly.[7]

Zlata's readers learn how it feels to lose friends—many escaping the war, others falling victims to mortar attacks. Life during wartime also means that time comes to a standstill and days go on forever:

> We're all waiting for something, hoping for something, but there's nothing. . . . Now these maps are being drawn up, separating people, and nobody asks them a thing. . . . Ordinary people don't want this division, because it won't make anybody happy—not the Serbs, not the Croats, not the Muslims. But who asks ordinary people? Politics asks only its own people.[8]

Zlata's Diary, which is often compared to the *Diary of Anne Frank*, reminds us all that war robs children of normal childhoods. A child who becomes a refugee sees the world through different eyes.

9

The Right of Refuge

Those who work with refugees and see firsthand the problems they face have made several recommendations on ways to protect the rights of refugees, as well as to prevent the causes of their flight. None of these is an easy answer. One recommendation, although it might solve one set of problems, may create others. Another may appear too idealistic and impractical. As we look at potential solutions, we must also ask questions. Who stands to gain and who to lose? Does a possible solution help refugees but also threaten the national interest of a host country? Each of the following recommendations will be discussed in terms of its strengths and weaknesses:

- increase aid available to refugees
- prevent refugee crises by treating the causes of forced migrations

- prevent forced repatriation (return of refugees against their will) by protecting the rights of the refugees to flee

- develop new institutions and strengthen existing ones so that they can better assist refugees

- ensure physical safety for all world citizens and support for human rights

Increase Aid Available to Refugees

The need is so great that many advocate increasing the amount of aid available to refugees. Recognizing that the world spends three times as much per day preparing for war as it does in a year protecting the peace, they recommend redirecting funds previously earmarked for building a strong military.[1] Aid could be used instead to support refugees as they integrate into a new society—meeting health needs, finding a school, learning a new language, securing a job, becoming accepted into the fabric of the community.

Increased aid would make it possible to better address the needs of women and children who account for 75 to 80 percent of uprooted people. Relief workers have recommended that women and children's health and education needs become a priority. They also stress the importance of making every effort to keep families together. Having witnessed the special difficulties children face in adapting to the confining life of a refugee camp, they advocate as much freedom of movement as possible.

Askalu Menkerios, a woman doctor and ambulance driver during the liberation struggle of Eritrea in eastern Africa, says, "Our first task is to spread literacy among women" so that they can learn to manage their own lives.[2] Medina, a refugee from Eritrea, wants to remember a saying that hung on the wall of a sewing center in a refugee camp in the Sudan: "I am called a refugee, but I have made that into a ministry of peace. We are women of courage. We have to swim rivers without perhaps knowing how to swim. Sometimes we take refuge because we want to own our own lives."[3]

Although some analysts agree that the need for refugee assistance is high, they also realize that governments of host countries have already overextended their budgets to accommodate refugees. This phenomenon is readily apparent in the United States. It has been reported that the federal government spent $709.3 million for the resettlement of refugees in 1992; the cost of resettlement for the state and local governments during that year reached $620 million. The California state refugee coordinator and the federal Office of Refugee Resettlement have determined that 53 percent of all refugees who settled in California after 1976 were still dependent on Aid to Families with Dependent Children and other welfare programs in 1992.[4] Massachusetts, Minnesota, and Wisconsin have also cited that more than 50 percent of their refugees are welfare-dependent. A Health and Human Services study in 1991 revealed that approximately 44 percent of refugees from the former Soviet Union were dependent on public cash assistance a year after arrival.[5] Recognizing the tremendous burden

A Somali student studies English at the Refugee Center in Washington, D.C.

placed on the taxpayers, many recommend a decrease in support by public agencies and an increase in aid from private agencies.

Prevent Refugee Crises by Treating the Causes of Forced Migrations

Economic imbalances, poverty, lack of job opportunities, environmental devastation, civil unrest and violence all contribute to displacement within and across borders. The international community needs to be made aware of impending crises in a timely fashion so that it can become involved in prevention. Robert S. Chen, professor at Brown University, points out that early-warning programs designed to monitor and forewarn of famines and other emergencies do exist, but they are not connected to the decision-making bodies in those countries that could provide aid.[6]

Preventing tragedies is far better in economic terms than curing them through hastily mounted relief operations, says Francis Deng. "Better foresight and longer-term planning would deprive emergency situations of their compelling urgency and reduce the sense of panic engendered by circumstances that are already out of control."[7] J. Brian Atwood, head of the U.S. Agency for International Development, commenting on the $35 million given to Rwanda in May 1994 to aid with the disaster following the mass slaughter, said, "One wonders if we had had that $35 million in the previous two years whether we could have done something to avoid the killing."[8]

Both those who work with refugees and those who wish to limit the number of refugees allowed to migrate agree on the paramount importance of taking preventive measures. Individuals and international organizations, however, differ on the methods used to achieve this goal. The question most often debated becomes, "How can one best ascertain what, if any, outside intervention is warranted?"

Francis Deng, representative of the secretary-general of the United Nations on internally displaced persons, explains that the international community must strike a delicate balance between motivating governments to care for their people and making it clear that if they do not, the international community will take a stand.[9] Although many favor protection for the internally displaced, others dismiss such a goal as impractical. Not only is each country responsible for its own people, but the resources, they say, are simply not available for the vast numbers of people who need help.

Speaking of the role of the international community, Hiram A. Ruiz, policy analyst for the U.S. Committee for Refugees, says,

> If there is conflict in the refugees' home country, it can seek to mediate. If a government is persecuting a minority group or the citizenry at large, it can be condemned—privately, publicly, and in international fora such as the U.N. Human Rights Commission, Security Council, and General Assembly. If condemnation has little effect, it can be targeted with sanctions, formal or informal.[10]

Ruiz clearly outlines a course of action that many would deem reasonable, but timing—when to move from one stage to the next—can be a subject of great dispute.

Kathleen Newland of the Carnegie Endowment for International Peace illustrates the difficulties in determining the best methods of preventing a refugee crisis. "Prevention, where possible, is the most effective form of protection for people in danger of becoming refugees," she writes. "It involves promotion of human rights, economic development, conflict resolution, the establishment of accountable political institutions, and environmental protection." Yet she also cautions against giving political support that will prolong the internal conflict and raise the level of violence:

> External intervention in local disputes often disrupts local traditions of bargaining and compromise by giving one party, clan, or faction a definitive upper hand. An outside patron may prop up leaders who have little if any domestic legitimacy, and give them the firepower to enforce their will.[11]

The international community must often choose between respecting national sovereignty on the one hand and, on the other, taking global responsibility. Brown University professor Robert S. Chen, speaking of the conflict between humanitarian priorities and the principle of sovereignty, asks, "What actions can be taken to protect human rights when a government refuses to cooperate or give access? To what degree should the human right to food take precedence over a state's authority to control its territory and those who live there?"[12]

An isolationist approach suggests that each country be allowed to work out its own problems. Humanitarian aid can be seen as a tool to promote not self-reliance but instead a relationship built on dependency. The principle of sovereignty dictates that nations must not interfere in the internal affairs of other nations. Only a real threat to international peace warrants such action.

Prevent Forced Repatriation by Protecting the Rights of the Refugees to Flee

A convention adopted by the United Nations gives refugees the right not to return to their country of origin against their will. Yet enforcing this principle, known as non-refoulement, requires making an often difficult determination of whether or not a person seeking asylum is truly a refugee fleeing from fear of persecution. Haitians, apprehended on the high seas before reaching land, were treated as economic migrants, not as refugees, and were sent back to Haiti. A young Guatemalan, to cite another example, fled from guerrillas who tried to recruit him at gunpoint and was then denied asylum by the U.S. Supreme Court. The Court ruled that he was not persecuted for his political opinion and therefore did not have the right to protection.

The Federation for American Immigration Reform (FAIR) cautions against a government policy that allows foreign nationals to enter the United States without proper documentation and remain there while applying for asylum. "Political asylum is now routinely used as a means to get around U.S. immigration laws."[13] The application process may take years; meanwhile, the applicant receives work authorization and access to public benefits. Ed Lytwak from Carrying Capacity Network contends, "Those that abuse the system by entering the country illegally or under fraudulent asylum claims are affecting the number of those who are truly in need and have legitimate claims."[14] FAIR and others would argue that a quicker, more efficient process of determining who should receive asylum must be established before refugees can be guaranteed the right of non-refoulement.

Develop New Institutions and Strengthen Existing Ones

The role of the International Committee of the Red Cross, a neutral organization, should be expanded, says James Ingram, former director of the UN World Food Program, "building on its strength as a neutral organization."[15] The U.S. Committee for Refugees advocates a thorough overhaul of the United Nations system, which would enhance representation and strengthen the decision-making processes of the Security Council. Francis Deng has suggested establishing the equivalent of the UN High Commission for Refugees for the internally displaced, or, alternatively, expanding the mandate of the UNHCR specifically to include the internally displaced. These proposals would give these institutions greater authority within the international community and allow them to aid a larger number of refugees.

These institutions, however, cannot be strengthened

without the establishment in host countries of a more efficient process to meet the rising number of applicants. In 1983, 100,000 people applied for asylum in Europe, North America, Australia, and Japan. Within ten years, the number had risen to 800,000. In Germany alone the number of applications went from 121,000 in 1989 to 438,000 in 1992. Kathleen Newland endorses "tough, fair, and fast determination procedures for asylum seekers, so that the system meant to protect refugees is not clogged with people trying to use it as a back channel for voluntary migration."[16]

John Martin, writing in *SCOPE*, a journal published by the Center for Immigration Studies, proposes scaling back the number of refugees allowed into the United States from over 119,000 in fiscal year 1993 to the original number of 50,000, cited in the 1980 Refugee Act, which outlines United States refugee policy. Martin also suggests easing the impact of refugees on certain states by limiting the number of new refugees to those states.[17] Such a system would ensure that more states, not a select few, share the responsibility.

Others advocate placing a ceiling on admissions of refugees. Simcox and Jenks, also of the Center for Immigration Studies, in an article entitled, "Refugee and Asylum Policy: National Passion versus National Interest," write, "In a truly effective ceiling, refugee and mass asylum emergencies requiring higher admissions would be offset by lower admissions of other categories of entrants in that year, such as immediate family members and professionals and skilled workers."[18]

Ensure Physical Safety for all World Citizens and Support for Human Rights

Of all the conditions that force people to become refugees, human rights abuses may well rank highest. Without freedom of movement within one's country, or to and from that country, without freedom of speech, religion, and dissent, without freedom from the fear of torture or political imprisonment, people will be driven to flight.

The United Nations and other organizations have reached the conclusion that a sovereign nation has human rights obligations; when these are violated, the international community must be held accountable. In the words of Larry Minear of the Refugee Policy Group, "Where gross human rights violations occur, sovereignty is, in effect, no longer sovereign."[19] Yet when a case calls for UN intervention, how does one determine the means to be used?

Lawrence Weschler, writing in *The New Yorker*, says, "Tyrannies all over the world exist in the ironclad certainty that people are nothing more than meat on bones. Anything that their subjects are or have beyond that exists at the sheerest whim of the regime." To counter tyranny, human rights monitors must stand watch around the world.

"How can mere vigilance, the puny insistence on the rule of law in the face of armored, historically entrenched tyranny, ever make any difference?" Weschler asks. When enough people insist forcefully on human rights, he declares:

Jewish refugee children on the deck of the *SS President Harding* prepare to disembark in New York City on June 3, 1939.

Then, over time, a light does begin to shine in the middle of the dark—a substantial light that not only illumines but actually begins to melt tyrannies. It's uncanny. But one should be clear about the nature of that light . . . It has always been people, sentries like these, witnessing and declaring the truth, who work that magic.[20]

Francis Deng has talked with refugees around the world. "The voices from El Salvador are just like the voices from the Sudan," he says. The hopes and desires are universal: freedom from hunger and a craving for peace. What is needed, Deng says, "is often a restored sense of dignity, not increased development. People who once had food and cattle never thought of themselves as poor."[21]

Only when human rights are no longer violated will refugees return to their homes. Not until human rights are upheld, will refugees stop their flight.

None of these recommendations is guaranteed to lead to a perfect solution. Examining different possibilities, however, may bring us closer to solving the problems of refugees. The struggle to prevent the forced migration of refugees while at the same time respecting the rights of all citizens will continue.

Sources for Information on Refugee Facts and Policy

American Friends Service Committee
1501 Cherry St.
Philadelphia, PA 19102
Quaker organization that supports conflict resolution through reconciliation and provides relief to refugees.

Amnesty International
International Secretariat/1 Easton Street
London WCIX8DJ
Great Britain
or
322 Eighth Ave.
New York, NY 10001
Supports human rights and works to free prisoners of conscience and offer them asylum.

CARE
151 Ellis St.
Atlanta, GA 30303
Responds to the needs of refugees and displaced persons in emergency situations.

Carrying Capacity Network
1325 G St. NW, Suite 1003
Washington, DC 20005-1003
Works to recognize the interrelated nature of environmental degradation, population stabilization, and resource conservation.

The Carter Center
One Copenhill
Atlanta, GA 30307
Helps countries resolve their internal conflicts in a peaceful manner, and encourages them to hold free and fair democratic elections.

The Federation for American Immigration Reform (FAIR)
1666 Connecticut Ave. NW, Suite 400
Washington, DC 20009
Works to reform immigration policy and restrict immigration to the United States.

Human Rights Watch
485 Fifth Ave.
New York, NY 10017
Monitors human rights practices of governments worldwide.

International Committee of the Red Cross
19 avenue de la Paix
CH-1202 Geneva, Switzerland
Protects and assists victims of international and civil wars.

International Rescue Committee
122 East 42nd St., 12th Floor
New York, NY 10168-1289
Started by Albert Einstein, this organization provides resettlement services and emergency relief.

Refugees International
21 Dupont Circle NW
Washington, DC 20036
Reports on refugees around the world and advocates fair refugee policy.

Save the Children Federation
54 Wilton Rd.
Westport, CT 06880
Provides assistance to refugees in areas of agriculture, health care, education, and literacy training.

United Nations Children's Fund (UNICEF)
3 UN Plaza
New York, NY 10017
Supports emergency humanitarian assistance and supports programs in nutrition, primary health care, and education to meet the needs of children.

United Nations High Commissioner for Refugees
Branch Office for the United States
1718 Connecticut Ave. NW
Washington, DC 20009
Provides protection for refugees and seeks durable solutions.

United Nations Relief and Works Agency for Palestine Refugees in the Near East (UNRWA)
U.S. Committee for Refugees
1717 Massachusetts Ave. NW
Washington, DC 20036
Provides assistance to Palestinian refugees.

Women's Commission for Refugee Women and Children
c/o International Rescue Committee
386 Park Ave. South
New York, NY 10016
Acts as a liaison between refugee women and children and foreign governments.

World Vision
919 West Huntington Dr.
Monrovia, CA 91016
Provides emergency disaster relief, child sponsorship, primary health care, agricultural development, and community leadership training projects throughout the world.

Worldwatch Institute
1776 Massachusetts Ave. NW
Washington, DC 20036
Encourages a sustainable society in which human needs are met in ways that do not threaten the environment or future generations.

Chapter Notes

Chapter 1

1. David B. Ottaway, "Mostar's Muslims 'Living Like Rats,'" *The Washington Post* (February 21, 1994), pp. A1, A20.

2. David B. Ottaway, "Million Adrift in Europe's Biggest Forced Migration Since WWII," *The Washington Post* (July 14, 1993), p. A14.

3. Reed Brody, "Early Warning, Early Action," *Human Rights*, no. 92 (April 1993), p. 8.

4. Women's Commission for Refugee Women and Children, "Who Is a Refugee?" undated fact sheet.

5. Roger P. Winter, "The Year in Review," in *World Refugee Survey* (Washington, D.C.: The U.S. Committee for Refugees, 1993), p. 4.

6. Sadako Ogata, "Note on International Protection," cited in Bill Frelick, "Preventing Refugee Flows: Protection or Peril?" *World Refugee Survey*, p. 7.

7. Bill Frelick, "Preventing Refugee Flows: Protection or Peril?" *World Refugee Survey*, p. 13.

8. John Martin, "U.S. Refugee Resettlement Policy Requires Rethinking," *SCOPE* (published by the Center for Immigration Studies), no. 14 (Spring 1993), p 1.

9. The Federation for American Immigration Reform, "What to Do about Refugees," issue brief (March 1993).

10. Paul Lewis, "Stoked by Ethnic Conflict, Refugee Numbers Swell," *The New York Times* (November 10, 1993), p. A6.

Chapter 2

1. Howard Greenfeld, *The Hidden Children* (New York: Ticknor & Fields, 1993), p. 29.

2. Ibid. p. 83.

3. Gay Block and Malka Drucker, *Rescuers: Portraits of Moral Courage in the Holocaust* (New York: Holmes and Meier, 1992), p. 18.

4. See Greenfeld, p. 111, for information on the First International Gathering of Children Hidden During World War II.

Chapter 3

1. United Nations High Commissioner for Refugees, *The State of the World's Refugees* (New York: Penguin, 1993), p. 11.

2. "Organization of African Unity Convention Governing the Specific Aspects of Refugee Problems in Africa," reprinted in *The State of the World's Refugees*, p. 165.

3. *The State of the World's Refugees*, pp. 171–172.

4. International Committee of the Red Cross, *1992 Annual Report* (Geneva: International Committee of the Red Cross, 1993), pp. 13–16.

5. Rob Gurwitt, "Back to the Melting Pot," *The Social Contract* (Fall 1992), p. 20. Reprinted from *Governing* (June 1992).

6. Sima Wali, "Uprooted Women and Hunger," in *Hunger 1993: Uprooted People* (Washington, D.C.: Bread for the World Institute on Hunger and Development, 1993), p. 55.

7. Randall A. Salm, "Refugee and Displaced Children: The Bitter Legacy of Conflict," in *Hunger 1993: Uprooted People*, p. 61.

8. *The State of the World's Refugees*, p. 174.

9. United Nations Children's Fund (UNICEF), *The State of the World's Children 1994* (Oxford: Oxford University Press, 1994), p. 56.

10. Ibid. p. 4.

11. Ibid. p. 38.

Chapter 4

1. Patricia Weiss Fagen, "Peace in Central America: Transition for the Uprooted," *World Refugee Survey* (Washington, D.C.: The U.S. Committee for Refugees, 1993), pp. 33–34.

2. Ibid. p. 35. For additional information, see "Country Report," *World Refugee Survey*, p. 144.

3. United Nations High Commissioner for Refugees, *The State of the World's Refugees* (New York: Penguin, 1993), p. 107.

4. *World Refugee Survey*, p. 145.

5. Fagen, p. 37.

6. Pamela Constable, "In Guantanamo Camps, Anxious Cubans Wait Indefinitely as Prisoners," *The Washington Post* (September 29, 1994), p. A33.

7. Larry Rohter, "Foreign Policy: Florida Has One," *The New York Times* (May 22, 1994), sec. 4, p. 1.

8. *The State of the World's Refugees*, p. 42.

9. "Haiti: Immigration Policy Dilemma," *Carrying Capacity Network Clearinghouse Bulletin* (July 1994), p. 3.

10. David Simcox and Rosemary Jenks, "Refugee and Asylum Policy: National Passion versus National Interest," *The Negative Population Growth Forum* (February 1992), p. 4.

11. "Haiti: Immigration Policy Dilemma," p. 4.

12. Don Barnett, "Their Teeming Shores," *National Review*, vol. XLV, no. 21 (November 1, 1993), p.55.

13. *World Refugee Survey*, p. 146.

14. *The State of the World's Refugees*, p. 42.

15. "Supreme Court Hears Haitian Challenge to 'Floating Berlin Wall,'" *Refugee Reports: A News Service of the U.S. Committee for Refugees* (March 31, 1993), pp. 2–5.

16. Ibid. pp. 3–5.

17. "Aristide's Talk: Yes to Reconciliation," *The New York Times* (October 5, 1994), p. A17.

Chapter 5

1. Donatella Lorch, "Rains and Disease Ravage Refugees Fleeing Rwanda," *The New York Times* (May 2, 1994), p. A10.

2. Keith B. Richburg, "Instant City of Misery in a Lush Land," *The Washington Post* (May 4, 1994), pp. A1, A31.

3. Keith B. Richburg, "From War to Living Hell—and Back to Uncertainty," *The Washington Post* (July 29, 1994), p. A1.

4. Andrew Cohen, "Humane Intervention Is Hell," *Village Voice* (January 19, 1993), p. 26, cited in Francis M. Deng, *Protecting the Dispossessed: A Challenge for the International Community* (Washington, D.C.: The Brookings Institution, 1993), p. 52.

5. *World Refugee Survey* (Washington, D.C.: The U.S. Committee for Refugees, 1993), p. 70.

6. Ibid. pp. 69–72.

7. See United Nations High Commissioner for Refugees, *The State of the World's Refugees* (New York: Penguin, 1993), pp. 92–93, for information on the processing center.

8. Ibid.

9. *The State of the World's Refugees*, p. 95.

10. Francis M. Deng, *Protecting the Dispossessed: A Challenge for the International Community* (Washington, D.C.: The Brookings Institution, 1993), p. 63.

11. Judy Mayotte, *Disposable People? The Plight of Refugees* (New York: Orbis, 1992), p. 253.

12. Ibid. p. 277.

13. *World Refugee Survey*, p. 74.

14. Ibid. p. 73.

15. Deng, p. 80.

16. Sadako Ogata, "Foreword," in Mayotte, *Disposable People?* p. xiii.

17. Mayotte, p. 277.

18. Lionel Rosenblatt, "Prompt Aid Can Avert Famine in Southern Africa," *International Herald Tribune* (June 2, 1992).

Chapter 6

1. United Nations High Commissioner for Refugees, *The State of the World's Refugees* (New York: Penguin, 1993), pp. 47, 50.

2. For information on the intifada, see Thomas L. Friedman, *From Beirut to Jerusalem* (New York: Farrar, Straus, & Giroux, 1989), pp. 384–387.

3. *World Refugee Survey* (Washington, D.C.: The U.S. Committee for Refugees, 1993), p. 102.

4. *World Refugee Survey*, p. 103.

5. Daniel U.B.P. Chelliah, "Middle East Hunger Update," *Hunger 1993: Uprooted People* (Washington, D.C.: Bread for the World Institute on Hunger and Development, 1993), p. 151.

6. *World Refugee Survey*, p. 105.

7. Ibid. p. 104.

8. Friedman, p. 444.

9. Ibid. p. 395.

10. *World Refugee Survey*, pp. 103–104.

11. Complete texts of Yitzhak Rabin and Yasir Arafat's speeches can be found in *The New York Times* (September 14, 1993), p. A12.

Chapter 7

1. See Judy Mayotte, *Disposable People? The Plight of Refugees* (New York: Orbis, 1992), pp. 168–171 for the story of Farida and Tajwar.

2. Ibid. p. 178.

3. Ibid. p. 159.

4. Ibid. p. 163.

5. *World Refugee Survey* (Washington, D.C.: The U.S. Committee for Refugees, 1993), pp. 88–91.

6. Mayotte, p. 206.

7. *World Refugee Survey*, p. 92.

8. Francis M. Deng, *Protecting the Dispossessed: A Challenge for the International Community* (Washington, D.C.: The Brookings Institution, 1993), p. 95. Also see Mayotte, p. 39.

9. Mayotte, p. 91.

10. Ibid. p. 93.

11. Deng, p. 102.

12. Ibid., pp. 103–104.

13. For details on the repatriation plan, see *World Refugee Survey*, p. 79.

14. United Nations High Commissioner for Refugees, *The State of the World's Refugees* (New York: Penguin, 1993), p. 105.

15. Ibid. p. 105.

16. *World Refugee Survey*, pp. 79–80.

17. Deng, pp. 105–106.

18. *World Refugee Survey*, p. 88

19. Statement of Lionel Rosenblatt, "Refugees International Protests Forced Repatriation of Rohingya Refugees from Bangladesh," *Refugees International Bulletin* (December 7, 1992).

20. *World Refugee Survey*, p. 78.

21. *The State of the World's Refugees*, p. 136.

Chapter 8

1. John Pomfret, "Not All Healing Hands Welcome in Sarajevo," *The Washington Post* (February 13, 1994), pp. A1, A26.

2. *World Refugee Survey* (Washington, D.C.: The U.S. Committee for Refugees, 1993), p. 114.

3. Ibid. p. 116

4. David Hoffman, "Israel Returns Favor to a Muslim," *The Washington Post* (February 12, 1994), p. A14.

5. Bill Frelick, "Preventing Refugee Flows: Protection or Peril?" *World Refugee Survey*, p. 9.

6. Nancy Soderberg, "Promises Clinton Kept," *The Washington Post* (May 25, 1994), p. A23.

7. Zlata Filipovic, *Zlata's Diary* (New York: Viking, 1994), p. 121.

8. Ibid. pp. 145–146.

Chapter 9

1. Mark Sommer, "Who Will Pay for Peace?" *The Christian Science Monitor* (February 19, 1992), p. 18, cited in Judy Mayotte, *Disposable People? The Plight of Refugees* (New York: Orbis, 1992), p. 6.

2. Judy Mayotte, *Disposable People? The Plight of Refugees* (New York: Orbis, 1992), p. 300.

3. Ibid. p. 287.

4. Don Barnett, "Their Teeming Shores," *National Review*, vol. XLV, no. 21 (November 1, 1993), p. 53.

5. Ibid. p. 53.

6. Robert S. Chen, "Hunger Among Refugees and Other People Displaced Across Borders," *Hunger 1993: Uprooted People* (Washington, D.C.: Bread for the World Institute on Hunger and Development, 1993), p. 35.

7. Francis M. Deng, *The Challenges of Famine Relief: Emergency Operations in the Sudan* (Washington, D.C.: The Brookings Institution, 1992), pp. 121–122.

8. Jennifer Parmelee, "U.S. Aims to Head Off Threat of an African Famine," *The Washington Post* (May 31, 1994), p. A13.

9. Personal interview with Francis Deng, January 11, 1994.

10. Hiram A. Ruiz, "Repatriation: Tackling Protection and Assistance Concerns," *World Refugee Survey* (Washington, D.C.: The U.S. Committee for Refugees, 1993), p. 24.

11. Kathleen Newland, "Refugees: The Rising Flood," *World Watch*, vol. 7, no. 3 (May/June 1994), pp. 10–20.

12. Chen, p. 33.

13. The Federation for American Immigration Reform, "Political Asylum—A Back Door for Illegal Immigration," issue brief (March 1993).

14. "Haiti: Immigration Policy Dilemma," *Carrying Capacity Network Clearinghouse Bulletin* (July 1994), p. 4.

15. Cited in Chen, p. 34.

16. Newland, p. 20.

17. John Martin, "U.S. Refugee Resettlement Policy Requires Rethinking," *SCOPE* (published by the Center for Immigration Studies), no. 14 (Spring 1993), p. 5.

18. David Simcox and Rosemary Jenks, "Refugee and Asylum Policy: National Passion versus National Interest," *The Negative Population Growth Forum* (February 1992), p. 5.

19. Cited in "Reforming the International Refugee Aid and Protection System," by the staff of the U.S. Committee for Refugees, in *Hunger 1993: Uprooted People*, (Washington, D.C.: Bread for the World Institute on Hunger and Development, 1993), p. 79.

20. Reprinted by permission; © 1994 Lawrence Weschler, "Sentries," *The New Yorker* (January 10, 1994), pp. 70, 72.

21. Personal interview with Francis Deng, January 11, 1994.

Bibliography

Books and Reports

Titles especially recommended for young people are marked with an asterisk (*).

Block, Gay, and Malka Drucker. *Rescuers: Portraits of Moral Courage in the Holocaust.* New York: Holmes and Meier, 1992.

*Carter, Jimmy. *Talking Peace: A Vision for the Next Generation.* New York: Dutton, 1993.

Deng, Francis M. *The Challenges of Famine Relief: Emergency Operations in the Sudan.* Washington, D.C.: The Brookings Institution, 1992.

————. *Protecting the Dispossessed: A Challenge for the International Community.* Washington, D.C.: The Brookings Institution, 1993.

*Filipovic, Zlata. *Zlata's Diary.* New York: Viking, 1994.

Friedman, Thomas L. *From Beirut to Jerusalem.* New York: Farrar, Straus, & Giroux, 1989.

*Graff, Nancy Price. *Where the River Runs: A Portrait of a Refugee Family, with photographs by Richard Howard.* Boston: Little, Brown, 1993.

*Greenfeld, Howard. *The Hidden Children.* New York: Ticknor & Fields, 1993.

International Committee of the Red Cross. *1992 Annual Report.* Geneva: International Committee of the Red Cross, 1993.

Mayotte, Judy. *Disposable People? The Plight of Refugees.* New York: Orbis Books, 1992.

United Nations Children's Fund (UNICEF). *The State of the World's Children 1994.* New York: Oxford University Press, 1994.

United Nations High Commissioner for Refugees. *The State of the World's Refugees: The Challenge of Protection.* New York: Penguin, 1993.

Articles

Arafat, Yasir, and Yitzhak Rabin. "Text of Leaders' Statements at the Signing of the Mideast Accord." *The New York Times* (September 14, 1993), A12.

Barnett, Don. "Their Teeming Shores." *National Review,* vol. XLV, no. 21 (November 1, 1993), 51.

Brody, Reed. "Early Warning, Early Action." *Human Rights,* no. 92 (April 1993), 8.

Chelliah, Daniel U. B. P. "Middle East Hunger Update." in *Hunger 1993: Uprooted People,* p. 148. Washington, D.C.: Bread for the World Institute on Hunger and Development, 1993.

Chen, Robert S. "Hunger Among Refugees and Other People Displaced Across Borders." in *Hunger 1993: Uprooted People,* p. 15. Washington, D.C.: Bread for the World Institute on Hunger and Development, 1993.

"Comment: The Same Boat." *The New Yorker* (January 10, 1994), 4.

Fagen, Patricia Weiss. "Peace in Central America: Transition for the Uprooted." *World Refugee Survey,* 33. Washington, D.C.: The U.S. Committee for Refugees, 1993.

Frelick, Bill. "Preventing Refugee Flows: Protection or Peril?" in *World Refugee Survey,* 33. Washington, D.C.: The U.S. Committee for Refugees, 1993.

Gurwitt, Rob. "Back to the Melting Pot." *The Social Contract* (Fall 1992). Reprinted from the June 1992 issue of *Governing.*

"Haiti: Immigration Policy Dilemma." *Carrying Capacity Network Clearinghouse Bulletin* (July 1994), 4.

Hoffman, David. "Israel Returns Favor to a Muslim." *The Washington Post* (February 12, 1994), A14.

Lewis, Paul. "Stoked by Ethnic Conflict, Refugee Numbers Swell." *The New York Times* (November 10, 1993), A6.

Lorch, Donatella. "Rains and Disease Ravage Refugees Fleeing Rwanda." *The New York Times* (May 2, 1994), A10.

Martin, John. "U.S. Refugee Resettlement Policy Requires Rethinking." *SCOPE, no. 14,* published by The Center for Immigration Studies (Spring 1993), 1.

Newland, Kathleen. "Refugees: The Rising Flood." *World Watch*, vol. 7, no. 3 (May/June 1994), 10.

Ottaway, David B. "Million Adrift in Europe's Biggest Forced Migration Since WWII." *The Washington Post* (July 14, 1993), A14.

————. "Mostar's Muslims 'Living Like Rats.'" *The Washington Post* (February 21, 1994), A1, A20.

————. "UN Aid Flight into Tuzla Ends 2 Years of Isolation." *The Washington Post* (March 23, 1994), A23.

Parmelee, Jennifer. "U.S. Aims to Head Off Threat of an African Famine." *The Washington Post* (May 31, 1994), A13.

"Political Asylum—A Back Door for Illegal Immigration." The Federation for American Immigration Reform issue brief (March 1993).

Pomfret, John. "Not All Healing Hands Welcome in Sarajevo." *The Washington Post* (February 13, 1994), A1, A26.

Richburg, Keith B. "Instant City of Misery in a Lush Land." *The Washington Post* (May 4, 1994), A1.

Rohter, Larry. "Foreign Policy: Florida Has One." *The New York Times* (May 22, 1994), sec. 4, p. 1.

Rosenblatt, Lionel. "Prompt Aid Can Avert Famine in Southern Africa." *International Herald Tribune* (June 2, 1992).

————. "Refugees International Protests Forced Repatriation of Rohingya Refugees from Bangladesh." *Refugees International Bulletin* (December 7, 1992).

Ruiz, Hiram A. "Repatriation: Tackling Protection and Assistance Concerns." *World Refugee Survey*, 24. Washington, D.C.: The U.S. Committee for Refugees, 1993.

Salm, Randall A. "Refugee and Displaced Children: The Bitter Legacy of Conflict." *Hunger 1993: Uprooted People*, 61. Washington, D.C.: Bread for the World Institute on Hunger and Development, 1993.

Simcox, David, and Rosemary Jenks. "Refugee and Asylum Policy: National Passion versus National Interest." *The Negative Population Growth Forum* (February 1992), 4.

Soderberg, Nancy. "Promises Clinton Kept." *The Washington Post* (May 25, 1994), A23.

"Supreme Court Hears Haitian Challenge to 'Floating Berlin Wall.'" *Refugee Reports: A News Service of the U.S. Committee for Refugees* (March 31, 1993), 2.

Wali, Sima. "Uprooted Women and Hunger." *Hunger 1993: Uprooted People*, 55. Washington, D.C.: Bread for the World Institute on Hunger and Development, 1993.

Weschler, Lawrence. "Sentries." *The New Yorker* (January 10, 1994), 72.

"What to Do about Refugees." The Federation for American Immigration Reform issue brief (March 1993).

"Who Is a Refugee?" Women's Commission for Refugee Women and Children (undated fact sheet).

Winter, Roger P. "The Year in Review." *World Refugee Survey*, 4. Washington, D.C.: The U.S. Committee for Refugees, 1993.

Index

362.8   Sawyer, Kem Knapp.
SAW   Refugees

DATE DUE			